THE STORY OF "G" TROOP,
ROYAL HORSE ARTILLERY

BY
MAJOR H. M. DAVSON,
ROYAL HORSE ARTILLERY

The Naval & Military Press Ltd

Published by
The Naval & Military Press Ltd
Unit 10 Ridgewood Industrial Park,
Uckfield, East Sussex,
TN22 5QE England
Tel: +44 (0) 1825 749494
Fax: +44 (0) 1825 765701
www.naval-military-press.com

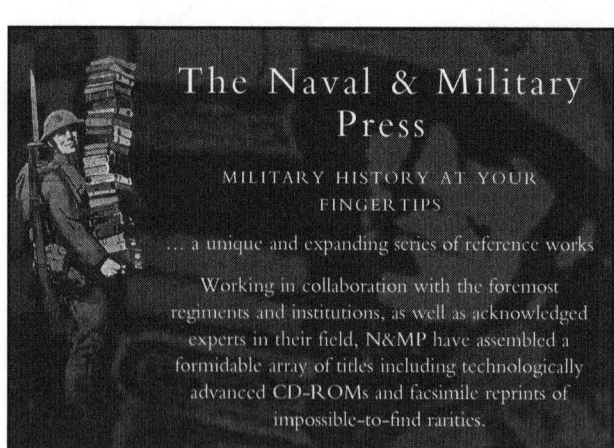

In reprinting in facsimile from the original, any imperfections are inevitably reproduced and the quality may fall short of modern type and cartographic standards.

INTRODUCTION.

THE following history has been compiled as far as possible from the battery records, which go back in detail to the commencement of the Mutiny when they were collected from the Troop Letter Book by Major General F. T. Whinyates, then commanding the Battery.

The account of the South American War has been taken from dispatches in the Public Record Office and from Miller's account of the campaign. For the Waterloo campaign I am indebted to Mercer's Diary and other published accounts and for the Mutiny, in addition to the records made by Majors Whinyates and Wickham, I have to thank Lt.-Genl. Sir Edwin Markham, Major General Arbuthnot and the late Major General Rideout for kindly reading the proofs and making additions and corrections.

The very full account given in the records of the South African War together with the help of the published works of the campaign made the compilation of that part of the history comparatively straightforward and Major General Bannatine-Allason and Brigadier General Mercer have kindly assisted me from their private notes made during the War.

Finally I desire to thank all those others either from recollection or from references have helped me on minor points, and especially one without whose assistance in collecting and making fair notes I could never have been able to finish the story in the time at my disposal.

H. M. DAVSON.

Ipswich,
    March, 1914.

NOTE.

This history of "G" Battery was completed and printed before the outbreak of war in 1914, but publication was held up with the idea of bringing it up to date at the close of hostilities.

As the war has been so prolonged, and sufficient data for writing an accurate account is not at present available, I have, in consultation with the present commanding officer (Major Eliott), thought it better to publish the book as it is, and hope that in the future somebody will be able to continue the history thus begun.

I should have liked to have finished the story of the battery which I took to France in 1914, but it would naturally take some time, and at present I have not the opportunities necessary for historical writing.

Some of the places mentioned with slight description are now familiar to many who will read this work, but they were not so when the story was written, and I hope that this may be borne in mind by those who read the book.

Many of those who so kindly helped one with the early history have now alas! been taken from us, as well as most of the officers who served with me in the battery, but I hope that there are still many in the regiment who will find some interest in the story of a famous troop.

H. M. DAVSON,
Lieut.-Colonel.

B.E.F.
Feby., 1919.

CONTENTS.

PAGE.

FRONTISPIECE.

"G" Troop at Waterloo. The charge of the Cuirassiers and Chausseurs of the Guard. (After the painting by Seccombe in the Battery Officers' Mess)

INTRODUCTION.

CHAPTER I.

Formation of the Battery—Buenos Ayres, 1807—Portrait of Captain Fisher (founder of the Battery)—Return of the Battery to England. 1

CHAPTER II.

The Waterloo Campaign: Belgium, 1815 8

CHAPTER III.

The Waterloo Campaign: Quatre Bras and Waterloo—Return to England, 1816—Map of Movements of "G" Troop during the Campaign. 14

CHAPTER IV.

The Indian Mutiny—Photograph of Lt.-Col. D'Aguilar (General Sir Charles D'Aguilar, G.C.B.) who commanded the Battery in the Mutiny—Map of Oude 25

CHAPTER V.

Home Service—The Fenian Rebellion 36

CHAPTER VI.

South Africa—Magersfontein—Portrait of Maj.-Gen. R. Bannatine-Allason, C.B., Commanding in South Africa, 1899 to September, 1900 39

CONTENTS.

PAGE.

CHAPTER VII.
The Ride to Kimberley—Bloemfontein 45

CHAPTER VIII.
Johannesburg and Diamond Hill 53

CHAPTER IX.
The Advance Eastwards—Brig.-Gen. H. F. Mercer, C.B., Commanding in South Africa from September, 1900, to the end of the war 60

CHAPTER X.
South Africa, January to end of the year 67

CHAPTER XI.
South Africa, the end of the war—Conclusion—Map of South Africa 85

List of Officers and Staff Sergeants of "G" Battery, R.H.A., with their Stations, from the Foundation of the Battery to the present time 94

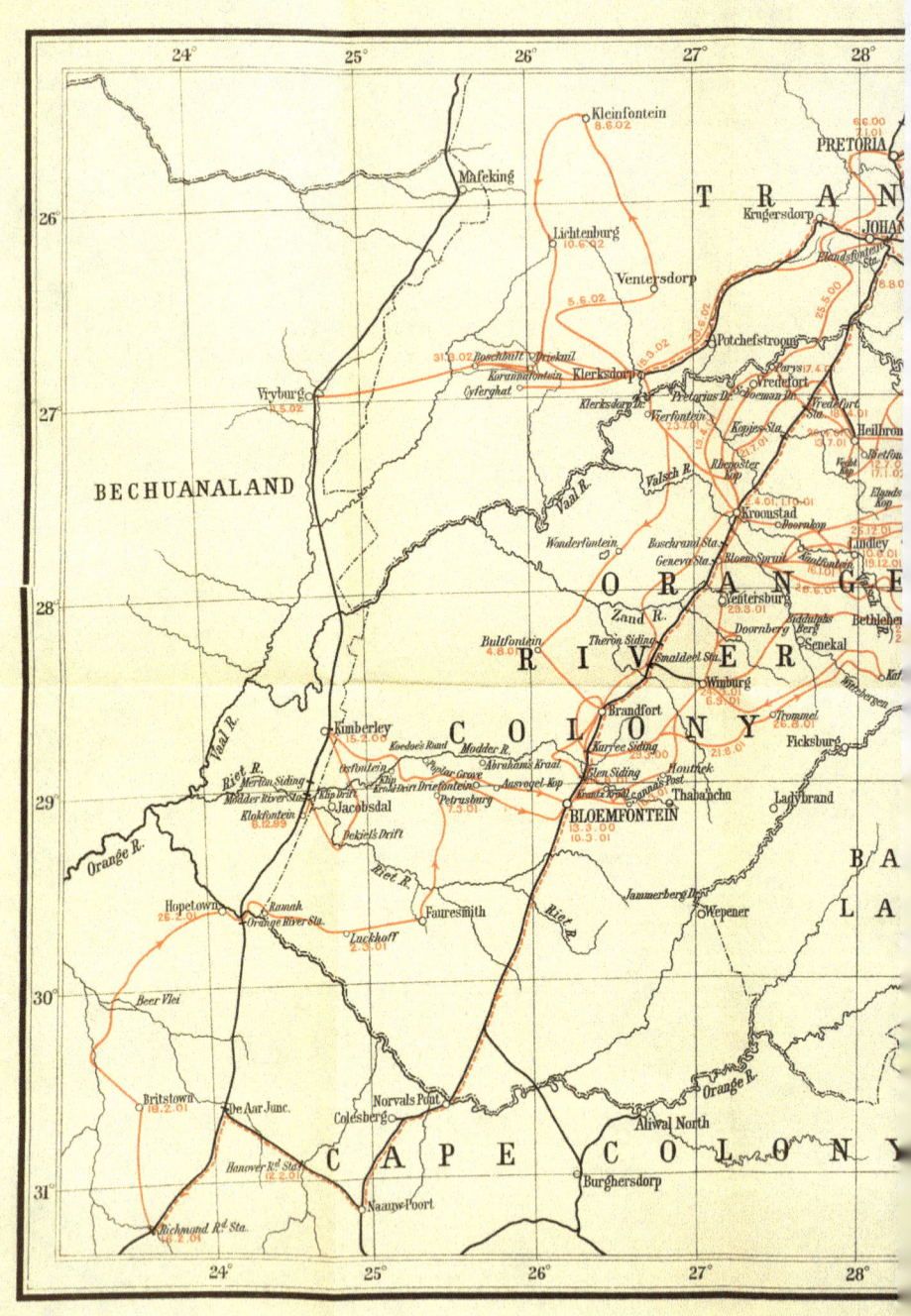

"G" TROOP AT WATERLOO.

The Charge of the Cuirassiers and Chasseurs of the Guard.
(After the painting by Seccombe in the Battery Officers' Mess).

THE STORY OF "G" TROOP, ROYAL HORSE ARTILLERY.

CHAPTER I.

THE formation of the Horse Artillery of the British Army dates from the year 1793.

The formation of G. Battery, Royal Horse Artillery dates from the year 1801 at which time divisions of A, B and C. Troops, which had been engaged in repressing the rebellion of 1798, were still quartered in Ireland. It was decided to form these into a new battery, and the intimation was first promulgated in the following letter dated, Woolwich August 20th, 1801:

Sir,

"I am authorised by the Master General of the Ordnance to apprise you that it is his lordship's intention to submit to his Majesty a proposal for founding a seventh troop of Horse Artillery."

"His Lordship upon reverting to the list of candidates for the appointment of a troop has been pleased to consider favourably of the pretensions of the senior captains, especially those now on Foreign duty, who appear to have additional claims on the score of hard service as well as seniority, but as the detachment you command at present* will by this arrangement become the principal part of the troop in question, he is willing to continue you in every respect as captain of it,

---

* A portion of "E" Troop.

until relieved in the charge by the officer he may judge proper to bestow it upon."

> I have the honour to be,
> etc., etc.,
> J. MACLEOD,
> D.A. General of Artillery.

Captain Fisher,
    Commanding R.H. Artillery,
        Mallow,
            Ireland.

The final order for the formation was dated November, and the troop was formed at Mallow, and remained there until the autumn of the following year when it moved to Woolwich. Captain Fisher then exchanged with Major Borthwick and succeeded to the command of his old troop.*

In 1803 Major Borthwick was promoted, and Captain (afterwards Sir Augustus) Frazer succeeded to the command. During the next three years the troop was quartered successively at Warley, Sevenoaks, Colchester, Wareham and Christchurch, and in March 1807 it was placed under orders for foreign service in South America.

BUENOS AYRES 1807.

In the spring of 1807 the British Government had decided on another expedition to South America. In the previous year a force under General Beresford had captured Buenos Ayres, but had been forced to retire to Monte Video, and Spanish irregular troops over-ran the country. Therefore, in order to secure the supremacy of British arms, and also with the fond hope of creating a diversion in Europe, a further force was ordered to the scene.

This force was placed under command of General Whitelocke, an officer then fifty years of age, who, having joined the 14th Foot in 1778 had proceeded to Jamaica with his

---

* This officer had a distinguished career as a Horse Artilleryman. As Major General Sir George Bulteel Fisher, K.C.B., he was Commandant at Woolwich 1827 and died there in 1834.

CAPTAIN FISHER.
(Major-General Sir George Bulteel Fisher, K.C.H.)
who formed the battery in 1801.

THE STORY OF "G" TROOP. 3

regiment four years later, and had there married a Miss Lewis of Cornwall, whose brother subsequently became Deputy Secretary at War, and to whose influence Whitelocke is said to have owed his advancement.

His appointment dated from the 24th February, and the troops already in the country were the 9th and 17th Light Dragoons and some troops of the 20th and 21st; one hundred and seventeen men of the Royal Artillery; the 38th, 40th, 49th and 87th regiments and detachments of the 54th and 95th. This force numbered 5,338 men in all, and was under the command of Brigadier General Sir J. Achmuty, who had served with Beresford in the previous year.

To augment this force Whitelocke was promised the brigade of General Crauford's which was then setting out for the Cape. It consisted of the 6th Dragoon Guards, the 5th, 36th, 45th and 88th regiments, the remainder of the 95th and 243 men of Royal Artillery making 4,212 in all.

As this force had actually sailed, and in case it could not be diverted in time, Whitelocke was given one troop of Horse Artillery, the 89th regiment and 500 recruits.

The Royal Horse Artillery (G. Troop) were dismounted, but complete with harness and appointments and were still under command of Captain Augustus Frazer. It totalled 6 officers, including a surgeon, and 183 men.

Whitelocke arrived in Monte Video in May and assumed command, but his reinforcements were detained by contrary winds and did not reach the mouth of the La Plata until the middle of June. Even then the weather was unkind, and it was not until the 27th that the force commenced to disembark at the Ensenada of Barragon, a small bay thirty miles east of Buenos Ayres. The cavalry and artillery were only partially mounted, for Whitelocke, in spite of all his efforts, which included sending vessels along the coast for the purpose, had been unable to collect sufficient animals for their requirements. It does not seem to have occurred to the powers at home to find out whether cavalry and horse artillery, shipped across the sea without horses, could be mounted at the seat of war, yet it should not have been difficult as despatches were passing regularly between Achmuty and the home government.

Before the disembarkation was finally completed at Ensenada, Whitelocke started his advance towards the city. The country was intersected with swamps and deep muddy rivulets and the march to Quilmer—twenty miles—occupied three days. The army was much exhausted and harassed by native cavalry and two guns had to be left behind, but there is no record of what battery they belonged to. Frazer at this time, in addition to his own battery, was in charge of twelve other guns—three pounders—which had been in the country before his arrival. Eventually the army reached the village of Reduccion, about nine miles distant from the bridge over the Rio Chuelo, on the opposite bank of which the enemy had constructed batteries and occupied what the general called "a formidable line of defence."

Frazer appears to have shelled the enemy out of the village and then the army prepared to force the passage of the river in two columns of which Whitelocke himself commanded one and Brigadier General Leveson-Gower the other. Colonel the Honourable T. Mahon, with G. Troop, the 17th Light Dragoons and the 41st regiment, held Reduccion as a sort of *point d'appui*.

On the 2nd July Leveson-Gower advanced to the river and found himself confronted by the Spanish General Liniers with 4,000 foot, 1,700 horse and 50 guns. Gower turned his flank and crossed at Paso Chico when the Spaniards retired with some loss. It may be of interest to artillery officers to learn that Gower had to leave some guns (3 pounders?) behind because he "found them unable to keep up with the infantry." Of course the country was to blame but the reason is not very clearly explained in the despatch.

On the same afternoon the right wing occupied the Miserere or western outlet of the city. Liniers attacked it at sunset but was defeated and fled leaving behind him thirteen guns. Whitelocke at this time was still on the Rio Chuelo and delayed marching into the city until the Spaniards had had time to

THE STORY OF "G" TROOP.   5

barricade it. He then lost another day in a summons to surrender, oblivious to the fact that Liniers had already refused to treat with Leveson-Gower. He then decided to storm it.

To do this he divided his force into separate columns and ordered them to march down the straight streets leading towards the river. Crauford and Pack were to move to the Plaza de Toros without firing a shot. Achmuty was to seize the Retiro, and two guns of G. Troop were ordered along the central street escorted by the carabiniers and three troops of the 9th Dragoons. The columns were unable to support one another and every house had been turned into a fortress defended by the troops, the inhabitants and their black servants. Crauford seized the Plaza and held it until 3.30 p.m. when he was obliged to surrender. Achmuty, with the 87th regiment, captured the Retiro and held it throughout the day, and the 45th performed the same feat at the Residency. The 88th regiment was annihilated and the survivors surrendered about 11 a.m. Knighton who commanded the guns and cavalry forced his way for some distance along the main street, but the hail of missiles and bullets from the house-tops was so severe, that, when he himself and his second in command were both severely wounded, and the passage of the guns stopped, he decided to withdraw. This was accomplished and the guns came into action against the hostile barricades at the entrance to the town where they did much damage. The general himself had remained with the reserve at the Miserere.

His position was now as follows. He had all the approaches to Buenos Ayres. His troops were in possession of the Retiro and Residence and the enemy had suffered two defeats outside the city and had permitted hostile columns to penetrate into their midst. Most generals would have been encouraged and contemplated ultimate and permanent success. It is true that Whitelocke had lost considerably but he had a strong reserve in hand, no guns had been captured and he had a troop of horse artillery practically untouched in a commanding position outside the town.

The nerve of the commander had however given way, and

when Liniers sent to propose that the British troops should retire from the town, and eventually from the country, if he gave up all his prisoners for whose safety, "on account of the excited state of the populace he could not be responsible," the Commander-in-Chief assented and agreed to forego the successes gained by his soldiers.

The troops were withdrawn to Monte Video and were gradually shipped to the Cape and to England until on the 9th September Monte Video was finally evacuated.

Whitelocke claimed in his defence that his Generals agreed with him on his plan of campaign, a somewhat weak plea for a Commander-in-Chief; that the inhabitants were hostile to British occupation, although he does not explain how he knew this; and that the occupation of Buenos Ayres would be of no use to England, a statement about a town which was to become the leading city of South America, and whose harbour was to command the major portion of the commerce of the eastern seaboard of the Continent, which places his political insight on a par with his military acumen. His strategy was at fault almost from the start; his orders for the attack were unworthy of a subaltern in a promotion examination; and his knowledge of the handling of artillery can only be described as elementary.

As an example of what he gave up by this surrender, he had in his pocket at the time a report from Frazer showing the captures of ordnance stores. They included 43 guns, 25,000 round shot and 11,000 shells for mortars. He had command of the sea, and the possession of Monte Video and the estuary of the River Plate, and support from a certain number of influential inhabitants. Against this he had lost 263 men killed, 540 wounded and 196 missing, which cannot be considered extraordinary out of a force of 11,180.

As far as the performances of the battery were concerned Whitelocke gave nothing but praise—indeed he gave their just due to all the troops—and of Frazer himself he wrote:—"I cannot sufficiently bring to notice the uncommon exertions of Captain Frazer, commanding the Royal Artillery, the fertility of whose mind, zeal and animation in all cases left difficulties behind."

The troop arrived at Cork in December, having lost nearly as many men on the voyage as it did in the attack on the city, but of course that may have been due to the deaths of wounded men.

Whitelocke was court-martialled on his return and removed from the army. The successes of Napoleon in Poland and the prospective results of the Peace of Tilsitt had taken the eyes of the British public off this minor expedition to South America but for many years there was a toast in the British army. "Success to gray hairs but not to white locks." One can only wonder if Napoleon and Benningsen had been so overcome by their losses of tens of thousands at Eylau and Friedland as Whitelocke was by his hundreds at Buenos Ayres, what changes it would have made in the Treaty of Tilsitt, or indeed if the meeting of the Emperors would ever have taken place.

In the next spring the troop was moved to Woolwich and in the following year to Woodridge where it remained until November 1814.

At this time Frazer, then a brevet Lieutenant Colonel was promoted and Lieutenant Colonel Sir Alexander Dickson, K.C.B. assumed command as Captain. The second Captain was Captain A. C. Mercer and the subaltern officers were Lieutenants Bell,* Hinks, and Ingilby.

* He was Adjutant of Horse Artillery during the Waterloo Campaign, commanded the Chestnut Troop in 1841, and as General Sir Wm Bell, K.C.B. died at Ripon in 1873

CHAPTER II.

THE WATERLOO CAMPAIGN: BELGIUM 1815.

In November 1814 the troop moved from Woodbridge to Colchester. It was still nominally commanded by Sir Alexander Dickson, at that time Q.M.G. at New Orleans, but in reality by Captain Cavalié Mercer, an officer who had seen service in South America, and, in accordance with British immemorial usage, it was in process of being reduced to the lower establishment, when the news arrived that Napoleon had landed at Golfe Juan.

To make the troop fit for service another unit in the barracks was broken up and all ranks worked with such a will that on the third day Sir Augustus Frazer, who was then C.R.A. at Colchester was able to report it in a condition to march. Lieutenant Leathes took the place of Lieutenant Bell who was appointed adjutant. On the 9th April the battery left Colchester for Harwich where it arrived at 3 p.m. and immediately commenced embarkation for Ostend. The operation was completed by noon next day and the vessels sailed on the following morning. It arrived at Ostend on Sunday 13th at 3 p.m. and landing at once commenced. The port authorities boarded the ship and commenced to throw everything overboard into the water. Men, horses and equipment were soaked but the prayers of the officers, who foresaw the ultimate loss of equipment due to darkness, beggars and a rising tide, were only met with the response:—"Duke's orders are positive. There is to be no delay in disembarkation." Mercer finally prevailed upon the naval port officer to leave the carriages on board for the night, but no military staff officer appeared with instructions as regards billetting, nor, in spite of diligent search, could one be found.

Finally, after men and horses had remained for some hours on the sands in torrents of rain, Mercer discovered some sheds

THE STORY OF "G" TROOP.   9

outside the town, to which, about 2 a.m. he succeeded in leading his starving and shivering troop.

On the 14th the carriages were disembarked by noon, and after waiting for four hours for the commissariat to supply rations, the battery mached off to Ghistel (a small village about six miles away), and next day, in fine weather, continued its march to Bruges where it was accommodated in the barracks. On the 16th it reached Ecloo a neat little village formed of two streets meeting in a market place where the guns were parked, and here the troop had its first view of Wellington who was *en route* from Brussels to Ostend. The Duke, who had previously given orders that no ammunition of any kind was to be parked in a village, scrutinised the battery closely but made no remark.

On the 17th, Ghent was reached, a town which was the head-quarters of the "army" of Louis XVIII, and as such was full of soldiers of every type and degree which made the arrangement of billets most inconvenient, and regiments arriving from England marched into the town halted a night and passed on into space nobody knowing where. Of the movements of the French they knew and heard little, which is not surprising as the Commander-in-Chief himself was ignorant of Napoleon's dispositions, and indeed it is doubtful if the emperor had finally decided on his plan of campaign. The battery spent seven days in Ghent during which time it found the royal guard for King Louis, a duty which seems to have been most popular with all ranks employed upon it. The visit was especially interesting for the officers who had the opportunity of meeting several French officers who had distinguished themselves in the great wars of the empire, but who had now decided to take sides against their old leader and follow the fortunes of the Bourbon King.

On the 25th, the troop left Ghent and marched along a very slippery road through Dendermonde to St. Gille, a move made in order to concentrate the cavalry division, the headquarters of which was at Ninove. The battery remained here for a week and then was suddenly ordered to move to Strytem, which, after a good deal of enquiry, proved to be a small village lying between Asshe and Brussels. Here Captain Mercer was informed that he was attached to Lord Edward Somerset's brigade, which consisted of the Life Guards, Greys, King's Dragoon Guards and Inniskillings. The attachment was little more than a name, however, for the battery was unable to join its brigade until the 21st June and then only for a few hours. It was at this time also that the 6 pounders which had served them in their previous campaign were replaced by 9 pounders and one 5½ inch howitzer. The change, if inconvenient, was fortunate, for it enabled the artillery to withstand the more powerful French guns on the 18th June. It was the opinion of more than one expert eye-witness, that, had the ordnance not been changed, the gunners would never have been able to hold their positions until the end of the day. What would have happened then could easily have been predicted.*

At this time Lieutenant Ingilby exchanged with Lieutenant Breton and joined E. Troop.

On the 29th May there was a grand cavalry review on the banks of the Dender near Grammont. The division was formed in three lines and numbered about six thousand men. The Duke of Wellington, it is said, was so struck with the appearance of the battery as it stood on parade that instead of moving across the front in the usual manner he rode round each subdivision, calling the attention of Blücher to "this beautiful battery" and receiving in reply from the veteran soldier "that there was not one horse in the battery that was not fit for a field-marshal."

* State of Battery 1st June, 1815   Horses.

5 guns (9 pr.) 1 5½ inch howitzer	48
9 wagons	54
1 spare wheel carriage	6
1 forge, 1 curricle, 1 baggage wagon	12
Draught horses	120
6 Detachments	48
2 Staff Sergeants, 2 Farriers, 1 Collar-maker	5
6 Officers horses (lent by Board of Ordnance)	6
6 Officers mules and baggage	6
Spare Horses	30
Chargers (including Surgeon)	11
	226

23 Non-commissioned officers and artificers 80 gunners, 84 drivers.   Total 187

THE STORY OF "G" TROOP. 11

The above remarks are taken from the diary of the commander of the troop and may perhaps be said to be prejudiced, but it is a fact that, according to an account published soon after the campaign, "the cavalry and horse artillery in passing through the Netherlands exacted universal admiration. The fineness of our horses and their equipments were far superior to anything they had ever seen; and the Jacobins were quite delighted to think that Bonaparte would soon be able to mount his dragoons on such fine horses. Indeed they did not hesitate to say, that the English might fight by sea because it was their element, but that our troops would not stand one hour against Bonaparte. *Our army was too showy to be good and our soldiers too civil to be brave."* *

The British army suffered from the causes which led to the last remark in more ways than reputation. The orders against putting the inhabitants to inconvenience were strict, and, in case of complaint, the Duke was always inclined to believe the representations of the country people in preference to the explanations of his own officers. The same thing had been noticed in the Peninsula. The idea that the inhabitants of a friendly country should be troubled as little as possible is, of course, excellent but it can be carried too far, and in this case the letters from mayors and landowners were undoubtedly given too great prominence. Our troops did practically no damage and complaints were numerous. Our allies the Prussians took or destroyed whatever they liked and never listened to complaints, which were in consequence few.

One instance occurred to Captain Mercer, after he had left the battery before Paris and joined his new troop, of a proprietor who complained to head-quarters that the Horse Artillery had stripped the lead off his roof and piping. The Duke without any enquiry ordered the battery to pay and it was in vain that Mercer protested that he had no knowledge of the occurrence. Finally after much time and great labour and the employment of a sort of secret service agency he was able to

* Dr. Halliday's account: Paris 1815. Quoted by Jones.

prove that the theft was committed by the French themselves and the order was allowed to lapse. It was never withdrawn.

No such incidents, however, occurred in the secluded village of Strytem where all ranks lived on the best of terms with the natives. The men were quartered in the village and neighbouring farms and the officers in the chateau. The horses were fed on the fat of the land, principally, apparently, on green clover but how they were kept fit is unknown; for there was no manœuvre ground in this intersected country and the roads were bad. But fit they were even after six weeks idleness as events were soon to prove.

On the 14th June Napoleon crossed the Sambre, on the day after Wellington had written that "his departure from Paris was not likely to be immediate," and it was not until 4 p.m., next day that Wellington was aware that a strong army was on his left front. The Duke then ordered a concentration.

At dawn, on the 16th, "G" Troop was suddenly ordered to move to Enghien where "Major McDonald would point out the bivouac for the night." Seeing that most of the officers were at the ball in Brussels, one division billeted separately and the baggage carts (local) not at hand the battery moved off in wonderfully short time. But on arriving at Enghien no Major McDonald appeared, whilst other corps arrived, and passed on without stopping, on the road to Braine le Comte. After waiting half an hour Mercer appealed to Sir Ormsby Vandeleur, whose brigade of cavalry had been halted inside the park, but the General told him he had nothing to do with him, neither had he any orders for himself. He then mounted his brigade and took the same road—"by instinct" Mercer surmises. As Vivian's brigade and Bull's troop followed—also without orders, —Mercer decided to follow on too. On arrival at Braine le Comte, 4 p.m., they attempted to give the horses a short feed, but before it was well begun the nosebags were taken off and the force moved on again. The men carried three days' rations but had had nothing since dawn, and the wagons had been outdistanced on the rapid march to Enghien. La Tour, beyond Braine, was blocked with the baggage of Hanoverian corps, and

THE STORY OF "G" TROOP.

the cavalry took to the fields leaving the battery to struggle through the crowded street and up the steep incline through the wood of Houssière, where the road was so bad that the carriages had to have double teams. On emerging from the wood the sound of cannon became apparent and all hurried forward. Major McDonald appeared and ordered Mercer to attach himself to Somerset's brigade, which the latter knew to be still in rear. He however pushed on to the Senne at Ronequières, and halted there to water his thirsty horses, until ordered by Sir Hussey Vivian to join his brigade of hussars and push on to the sound of the guns. The brigade advanced at a trot, until, at the entrance to Ninelles the troop halted to prepare for action. Then they hurried forward again past a crowd of fugitives, wounded men, frightened natives and inquisitive sightseers until, at dusk, as the firing began to slacken, they passed into the zone of shot and shell on the field of Quatre Bras.

Owing to the number of cross roads to the north-east of Brussels it is not easy to give the exact distance that the battery covered on this march, but it may be not far from the truth if we take it as thirty-eight miles. And this was accomplished between 7 a.m. and 9 p.m., over a road at times very bad and more than once blocked with stragglers and baggage. That the battery should have marched from Strytem to Braine, about 27 miles, without any definite order is perhaps surprising, but it must be remembered that Wellington had refrained from committing his corps from any movement until he was sure of the direction of Napoleon's attack. Ney's advance on Gosselies and Genappe, coming as it did in the nature of a surprise, would have congested the staff work and an isolated battery may well have been overlooked. It is curious, however, that whole cavalry brigades should have advanced from Enghien to Nivelles without any orders as to where they were to go, or what they were to do when they got there.

CHAPTER III.

THE WATERLOO CAMPAIGN.
QUATRE BRAS AND WATERLOO.

The battle of Quatre Bras was practically over when the troops arrived upon the scene, and drove over a terrain strewn with corpses until they reached the now famous cross roads, beside which they were ordered to bivouac for the night. Drawing water from a neighbouring well and cutting wheat from a field, they did the best they could for the horses and lay down to enjoy a well earned repose. It was not to be for long, however, for before dawn the firing broke out anew and the French troops beyond Frasnes commenced a forward movement.

Blücher's defeat at Ligny had made the present position impossible and the order to retreat was given. Mercer's orders were to follow one of the infantry corps, but McDonald who brought the order added "Major Ramsay's troop will remain in rear with the cavalry to cover the retreat; but I will not conceal from you that it falls to your turn to do this if you choose it." The battery commander promptly accepted this offer and the troop remained in the advanced position near the farm of Quatre Bras whilst the various corps concentrated near it and then moved off in the direction of Brussels.

It was at this time that the battery met its real commanding officer, Sir Alexander Dickson, who had just returned from New Orleans to take up a staff appointment. It was but a flying visit, however, and then he passed away once more. Shortly afterwards the ammunition wagons, which had rejoined during the night, were ordered back along the Brussels road and the guns remained with a thin screen of cavalry watching the French army, motionless to their front. About noon the troop was quite alone beside the farm of Quatre Bras, the only living creatures in sight being a picket of hussars near Frasnes, and Sir Hussey Vivian's brigade about two miles away to the left.

THE STORY OF "G" TROOP.   15

But although there was no life, around the battery the dead lay thickly strewn, for it stood near the spot where Kellermann had hurled his Cuirassiers against Pack's brigade in his fierce endeavour to break through the line, and it was here that the 42nd and 92nd suffered so severely.

The French line now advanced and the battery fired a salvo and rapidly retired. It was at this moment that there burst over the country that terrible storm which was such a noticeable feature of that day, when the war of elements triumphed over the struggle of man. "There instantly followed an awful clap of thunder," wrote Mercer, "and lightning that almost blinded us, whilst the rain came down as if a water spout had broken over us. Flash succeeded flash, and the peals of thunder were long and tremendous; whilst as if in mockery of the elements the French guns still sent forth their feeble glare, and now scarcely audible reports—their cavalry dashing along at a headlong pace adding their shouts to the uproar. We galloped for our lives through the storm striving to gain the enclosures about the houses of the hamlets, Lord Uxbridge urging us on, crying "Make haste! Make haste! For God's sake gallop or you will be taken!"

Fortunately the storm had somewhat bewildered the pursuers and caused the pursuit to slacken presumably in the village of Bauterlez. The French cavalry, that is to say Colbert's brigades, galloped round the gardens, and Lord Uxbridge led the battery off the main road into a narrow lane, which was found to be blocked at the far end by a body of Chasseurs. To reverse by unlimbering was the only thing to do, and wonderful to relate, it was done before the enemy quite knew what was happening. Thereafter the troops regained the chaussée and galloped down it amongst disorganised cavalry, in the drenching rain which nearly blinded friend and foe alike and made even near objects almost invisible. At Genappe the pursuit ceased as the pursuers had apparently lost touch of affairs in the darkness. It must indeed be considered an unlucky storm for Napoleon, for, not only did it hinder the French pursuit from Quatre Bras but it seriously interfered with Grouchy's march from Ligny. The French columns were all on the march and so suffered more than their enemies who for the most part had already reached their bivouacs. The cavalry moreover were under the impression that they were performing the familiar operation of hustling a flying foe and treated the pursuit with a levity for which there was no valid reason.

Having passed through the town of Genappe the battery was suddenly recalled to the southern edge to support the light cavalry. The French had again attacked and brought up some artillery to which "G" Troop replied, until they had exhausted all their ammunition when Captain Whinyates' Rocket Troop took up the fire.* The rockets, however, did not have much effect on the enemy, who continued their advance and forced the rear-guard cavalry on to the heels of the infantry until they reached the position of Mont St. Jean. Mercer had regained possession of his ammunition wagons in the retreat, and, when he arrived at the gravel pit near La Haie Sainte, he was able to return the enemy's fire and received support from the artillery of the main army. After a time the French fire slackened and the battery was able to withdraw behind the ridge to a sodden bivouac near the farm of Mont St. Jean. Horses were fed— there was no need of water—but officers and men had neither food nor drink, nor the wherewithal to light a fire. Before dawn a bombardier, who had been despatched towards Brussels to seek out the reserve ammunition, returned to report success in his search, and his arrival was all the more welcome because he brought a quantity of meat and biscuit which he had gathered from overturned wagons on the road, so that, during the long pause which ensued before the French attack, the famished men were able to prepare themselves for the fatigues of the day. Then the battle commenced. For a time the troop remained without orders, but as the commander found the firing growing in intensity, and the neighbouring units one by one leaving their bivouacs, Mercer decided to move his battery to a more forward position and advanced up the main road. He was promptly ordered back and retired to the position by the farm

* This was the first occasion on which these two batteries met. They supported each other continuously throughout the South African War, and are now (1914) brigaded together as the "V" Brigade, R.H.A.

THE STORY OF "G" TROOP.   17

of Mont St. Jean with its left on the main road where it remained for some time subjected to a grazing fire of shell which came over the main ridge. Soldiers in more modern warfare are used to being fired at from foes unseen, but in the days of Wellington, such a position was unusual and not borne with same equanimity, and to be killed in solitude by missles fired by unseen hands does not appear to have fulfilled the ideal of glory sought for by the personnel of the troop.

The times of movements of the units on the battlefield now became uncertain. The accounts are conflicting and we can only judge roughly by the sequence of events. Mercer himself confesses to ignorance of the actual time of movement. Certain it is however, that, after the first attack on Hougoumont, Bull's troop was moved up to the centre of the second line to support the artillery fire against the French in the enclosure. Ramsay and Webber-Smith were moved up on Clinton's right possibly to form some support against the cavalry which Napoleon was massing on his left. Then Ramsay replaced Bull who had had to retire to refit, and it must have been about 2 p.m., that "G" Troop was moved to a position on the right of the second line between Hougoumont and Merbe Braine facing a "formidable looking line of lancers drawn up opposite" which was threatening the right flank of the army. These were Piré's cavalry of the 2nd corps, with a light battery which opened fire on the troop. As Mercer was also being annoyed by fire from some howitzers on the French left centre, he ventured to open fire, but was immediately subjected to a deluge of shell from hitherto concealed batteries of more powerful calibre which obliged him to cease fire when the enemy did the same.

About 3.15 p.m., Hougoumont burst into flames, the French cavalry attacks were launched against the right and centre, and Wellington ordered up his only remaining artillery namely the troops of Bull and Mercer.* "They advanced with an alacrity

---

* Mercer gives this time as "about 3 p.m." It must however have been later than this.

C.

and rapidity, most admirable," stated one eye witness, and Mercer also wrote that they "flew as steadily and compactly as if at a review," whilst Wellington himself, who was getting anxious about the appearance of the troop, when he saw them crossing the fields at a gallop, led by Sir Augustus Frazer, who had taken the order, turned to his staff and cried out "Ah! that's the way I like to see horse artillery move."

As Sir Augustus Frazer galloped along he shouted to Captain Mercer, Wellington's instructions. The battery would probably be charged as soon as they reached their position, "but the Duke's orders are positive that in the event of their persevering and charging home you do not expose your men, but retire with them into the adjacent squares of infantry." He then pointed out the position, between two squares of Brunswick infantry, and left them.

And the cavalry did charge. It was no mediocre attempt of raw conscripts or amateur soldiers or half trained horses. The army of Napoleon in 1815 was, for its size, the best he had commanded for ten years: the men were all French; they were all veterans; they regarded their leader with a faith amounting to veneration; and the cavalry were the flower of the army and were led by such heroes as Ney, Milhaud and Kellerman.

To describe what followed one must borrow from the vivid description the great French writer who lived in their time and whose feelings were those of the men who lived and died in the charges.

"Gigantic men on colossal horses; helmets without plumes and cuirasses of forged steel; pistols in wallets and long sabres. Ney drew his sword and put himself at their head. The huge squadrons quivered. Then one saw a fearful spectacle. All this cavalry, swords raised, standards and trumpets in the air, formed in column of divisions.

With one movement, like that of a single man, and with the precision of a bronze ram that forces a breach, they descended the hill of La Belle Alliance, and hurling themselves into the bottom where so many men had already fallen, disappeared into

THE STORY OF "G" TROOP.

the smoke. Then, issuing from the shadow they reappeared on the far side of the valley. Always compact, swinging onwards at full trot through the storm of missiles, mounting the horrible muddy slope of the plateau of Mont St. Jean, they surged upwards grave, menacing, imperturbable. In the interludes of musketry and artillery one can hear the thunder of hoofs. They cross the battle like a monster: nothing has been like it since the heavy cavalry took the great Redoubt at Moscow. Murat is absent, but Ney is there. Each squadron sways and swells as the coils of a polypus. One can see them through a vast smoke that is torn into fragments. There is a confusion of casques, cries, sabres and horses quarters bobbing up and down in the midst of the hurly-burly .... Behind the edge of the plateau, in the shelter of the masked batteries, the English infantry formed in thirteen squares, aiming at what is about to appear, wait calm, silent, immovable. They do not see the cuirassiers and the cuirassiers do not see them; they listen to this sea of men; they hear the crescendo of 3,500 horses, the regular thunder of hoofs, the rumble of cuirasses, the clank of sabres and the sound as of a fierce, wild wind.

There was a terrible silence. Then suddenly a long line of raised arms brandishing sabres appeared above the crest; casques, trumpets, standards and thousands of faces, with grey moustaches, shouting "*Vive l'Empereur.*" All this cavalry poured on to the plateau and it was like the birth of a hurricane."

And the troop met it. As the guns unlimbered and opened fire the front rank of the enemy was barely a hundred yards away and continuing its advance. Mercer looked at the Brunswick squares. Yesterday in the retreat he had seen them throw away their arms and flee from the sound of the hoofs of their own cavalry: to-day they were standing but unsteady. He ignored the Duke's order and stood to his guns. The effect on the enemy was terrible. The whole front rank was practically thrown down and the column facing the battery descended from trot to walk, from walk to halt; and then the leading troopers turned and forced their way to the rear, until finally the whole mass retired over the crest of the hill, whilst a cloud of skirmishers took their place and fired at the battery with carbines and pistols at a range of forty yards.

Again the cavalry came on. "The spectacle was imposing," wrote Mercer, "and if ever the word sublime was appropriately applied it might surely be to it. On they came in compact squadrons, one behind the other, so numerous that those in rear were still behind the brow when the head of the column was but some sixty or seventy yards from the guns. Their pace was a slow but steady trot. None of your furious galloping charges was this, but a deliberate advance at a deliberate pace, as of men resolved to carry their point. They moved in profound silence and the only sound that could be heard from them amidst the incessant roar of battle was the low thunderlike reverberation of the ground beneath the simultaneous tread of so many horses."

The battery, with tubes in the vents and port fires spluttering, stood waiting for the word of its commander to hurl destruction into the ranks once more. At the word "fire" the same performance was repeated. Practically the whole front rank fell and the case shot carried destruction into the mass, until, from the very muzzles of the guns, the survivors retired crushed and bleeding over the hill.

Rallied by leaders tried in a hundred fights, once more they came forward, but the charge was not like those that had gone before and was easily repulsed.

It was the last charge of the day; the charge which supported the last infantry attack, and now the British infantry began to move slowly forward through the heavy ground. But the old guard was yet to attack and the artillery which supported it took heavy toll of the exhausted battery. "The rapidity and precision of the fire was appalling. Every shot almost took effect and I certainly expected we should all be annihilated." Not only the guns suffered but the limbers, which had been retired down the slope, received their share. Horses were knocked over like ninepins and the drivers could scarcely extricate themselves from their dead steeds. The gunners were so exhausted that they could not run the guns up after firing so, they got further and further back on to the limbers and wagons. Added to which, as one section was firing towards the left, the guns recoiled into a heap which increased the confusion. "The whole live long day," wrote Mercer pathetically, "had cost us nothing like this. I sighed for my poor troop—it was already but a wreck."

Of two hundred horses, one hundred and forty were dead or dying and the gunners who were left were so exhausted that they could not work the guns, and when the battle was over they threw themselves down in the wet and blood-stained mud beside the carriages. All three subaltern officers were wounded and when the order came to advance and support the final infantry attack it could not be obeyed. So they spent the night amongst the dead and dying on the position they had defended so well. The battery fired 700 shot per gun and Sir Augustus Frazer said afterwards, "he could plainly distinguish the position of "G" from the opposite ridge from the dark mass which even at that distance formed a remarkable feature in the field."

Lieutenant Hinks was wounded in the breast, Lieutenant Leathes in the hip; Captain Mercer's horse received eight wounds, and Lieutenant Breton had three horses killed under him.

Mercer describes the second charge as being led by an officer in a rich uniform covered with decorations, whom he heard afterwards was Ney. This must be incorrect as Ney was in the centre of the charge and was seen by many dismounted in an abandoned British battery. This was not "G." A Frenchman in the attack wrote that through the smoke he saw the English gunners abandon their pieces *all but six guns stationed under the road* who kept firing with grape and mowed the cavalry down.

It is not perhaps out of place to conjecture what would have happened if Mercer had retired his men and trusted to the Brunswickers to save the line. "That day when you saved the Brunswickers," a remark afterwards made to him at Woolwich, would not have come to pass, and Milhaud's cuirassiers would have made a hole in the line. What would have happened then can be left to the imagination—if imagination were needed. For those familiar with the character of Milhaud the probable result can be read in history.

The battery spent the greater part of the next day on the battlefield. They collected stray horses which were still fit for work and harnessed them to the vehicles, sent the spare carriages to Lilois and replenished ammunition from Waterloo. The baggage wagons arrived from Strytem bringing much needed provisions and about three o'clock, Mercer was able to move his troop from the neighbourhood of the dead and dying, to breathe the fresh air of a bivouac out of sight and sound of the field where he and his command had gained much honour.

Next day—the 20th—they passed through Nivelles. The little town was blocked with troops, wagons, camp followers and sight-seers, and it was some hours before the battery was able to clear the place and reach an uncomfortable bivouac near Haine. From here Hinks, whose wound was severe, was ordered back to take charge of the unhorsed carriages, and orders were once more given to join up with Lord Edward Somerset. This was accomplished next day, and for the first time since the commencement of the campaign the battery was united to its own brigade.

The French armies were now collecting at Avesnes and Philippeville, whilst the British army marched forward via Mons and Binche. That night was spent by "G" troop in a wet bivouac near Malplaquet, and next day it marched to Bavai where it halted whilst the situation was cleared up round Maubeuge. Wellington was at Cateau Cambresis, Blücher at Catillon-sur-Sambre and Soult with 20,000 men, at Laon. It became a question of marching past Soult and leaving a force to contain him and either by reason of the necessary countermarching which was thus entailed, or by bad staff work in the advancing columns, the congestion on the roads became so great that Somerset, to escape from the toils, led his brigade straight across country leaving the battery once more isolated to find its way to Cateau. By the use of country roads the commanding officer had almost succeeded in accomplishing this feat when the order was given to return to Forêt as the immediate neighbourhood was unsafe. The battery therefore turned about, but owing to the block in the roads could get no further than Montay, where it passed the night in the churchyard and next day it retired still further to Forêt on account of trouble at Landrecies, a town situated on the left of the advance, the commandant of which had refused to surrender. Cambray on the other flank, was captured on the 24th by the 4th Division.

On the 25th, the troop renewed its southward journey, and performed a wearisome march along roads choked with baggage wagons and stragglers until it arrived at the village of Escars. (Fresnoy). Next day the march was continued with the same inconveniences to Etreilles and on the 27th they crossed the Somme near Nesle, a town of some interest to Englishmen as being the birthplace of Blondel, the faithful troubadour of Cœur de Lion, and billetted in Goyencour. Soult at this time had been joined by Grouchy, and the two had fallen back from Laon to Soissons. An attempt of Grouchy to seize the bridge over the Oise at Compiegnes, had been forestalled by the Prussians and the two French Marshals, after having on the 29th fought an unsuccessful rear-guard action at Villars Cauterets, fell slowly back towards Paris. That night the battery spent at Verneuil. Next day it moved on to Chenevière where a halt was made which allowed the carriages, which had been left behind at Waterloo, to rejoin once more.

On the 3rd July, in full expectation of taking part in another battle, the battery advanced in company with Bull's troop. The two commanding officers, in their anxiety to get forward, made use of a bye road which separated them from the other corps and brought them to the advanced position at Blanc Mesnil near St. Denis, from which position they were obliged to retire to a safer billet at Garges. No fighting took place on this part of the encircling line, but on the other side of Paris, Vandamme attacked the Prussians at Issy and a somewhat bloody fight ensued. It was the last of the campaign, for on the same day Wellington, Blücher and Davout, signed the Convention of Paris and the star of Napoleon finally set.

On the 8th July the battery quitted Garges, and marching through St. Denis, crossed the Seine at Argenteuil on a very insufficient pontoon-bridge, which Wellington had caused to be constructed on the 2nd in order to gain touch with Blücher, who was at Versailles. The troop now ended its warlike career for a time and went into cantonments in the village of Colombes.

On the 18th Major Wilmot assumed command of the battery and Captain Mercer left it on appointment to "D" Troop, lately commanded by Bean and now by Lloyd, who had been dangerously wounded and was incapable of duty. One cannot but feel the greatest sympathy with this gallant officer in having to leave the battery which he had commanded so well, in order to assume a temporary command of a battery which was not highly thought of and which was reduced in 1816 to lie in abeyance for 74 years.*

So ended the Waterloo campaign. The battery remained at Paris until the 19th December and then marched via Beaumont, Noailles Beauvais to Grandvilliers where it passed Christmas Day.

On New Year's Day 1816 Poix was reached. Seven days later it arrived at Airaines, and on the 22nd it once more crossed the Somme, this time at Abbéville. It finally reached Calais on the 25th and next day went into quarters at Canterbury after an absence from England of nine and a half months. It was then removed to Woolwich. The subalterns, non-commissioned officers and men of the Horse Artillery batteries who had fought at Waterloo were granted two years service by General Order dated 15th September, 1815. The three subaltern officers, as well as Surgeon Hitchings, retired from the service soon after the campaign. Ingilby lived to become a General and a K.C.B.

* Vide Appendix II: Mercer.

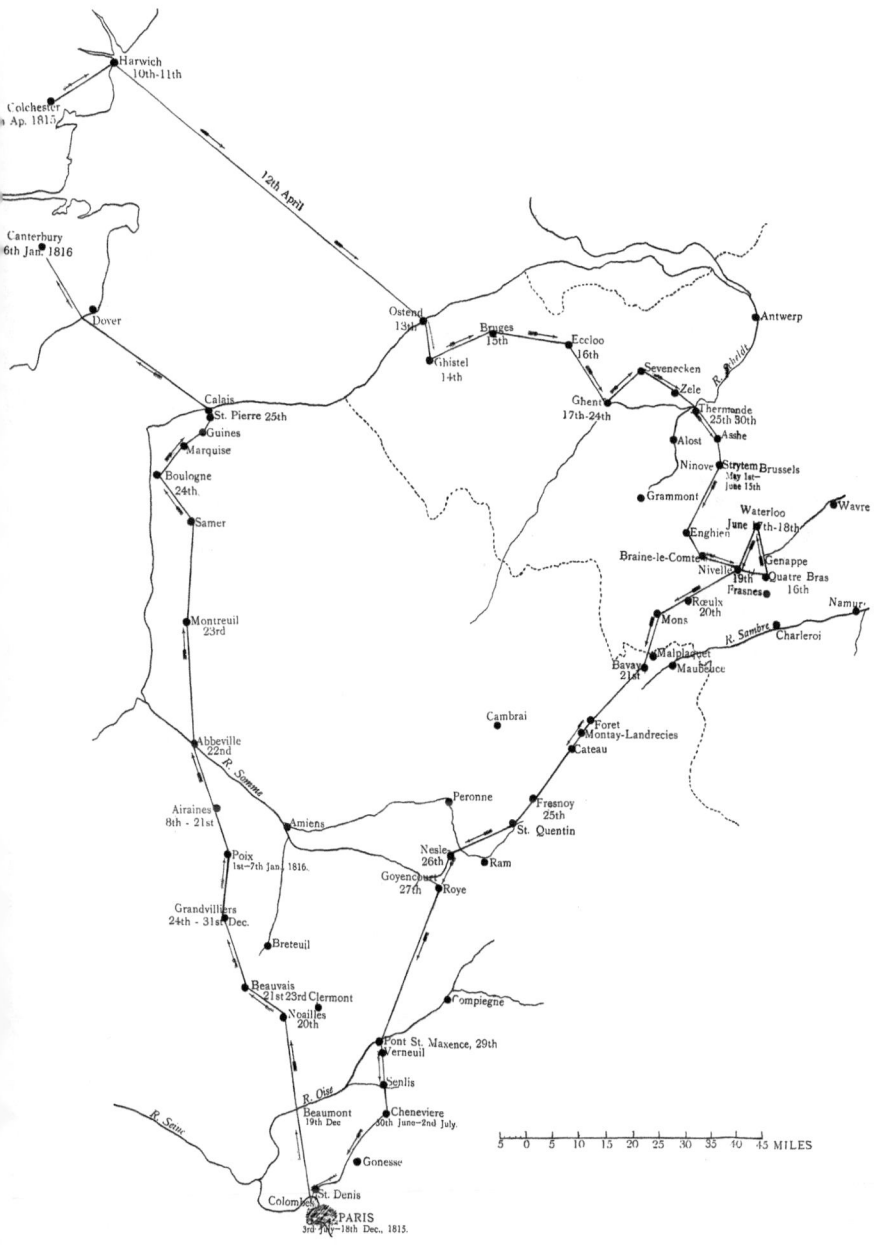

THE STORY OF "G" TROOP. 25

CHAPTER IV.

THE INDIAN MUTINY.

In 1817 the designation was changed to "F" Troop and next year, on the reduction of the Horse artillery, the Troop, which then consisted of two guns, was sent to Glasgow.* In 1822 it was transferred to Leith, and two years later returned to Woolwich.

The Troop then spent three years in Ireland and returned to Woolwich in 1829, when it sent two guns on detachment to Bristol. After a few months spent at Leeds and Newcastle it returned to Ireland in 1837, and was transferred to Woolwich in 1841. On the 21st January 1842, it marched from Woolwich via Kingston, Staines and Egham, under the command of 2nd Captain Holcombe and assisted in firing a salute at Bachelors Acres on the occasion of the christening of H.R.H. the Prince of Wales, on 25th January. It was again sent to Leeds and Newcastle, returned to Ireland in 1849, and back to Woolwich in 1853, having had twenty-one different stations since it returned from France.

The Troop at this time was commanded by Captain Walter Gilbert who had a great reputation as a horse-master, and his command was entirely horsed by Irish horses. He was promoted during the Crimean war and Brevet Major Colville Young, from the Crimea, was appointed to the command. This officer arrived at Portsmouth, went to a hotel and committed suicide by throwing himself from a window on 24th February 1855, and Brevet Major Charles D'Aguilar,† took command in his place. This officer had not yet returned from the Crimea, and the battery

---
* The establishment of Horse Artillery at this time consisted of five Officers, 10 Non-commissioned officers, 47 Gunners, 18 Drivers and 36 Horses.

† Lieutenant General Sir Charles D'Aguilar, G.C.B.

was temporarily commanded by Captain Leopold Paget. The subaltern officers were Lieutenants W. H. Goodenough, H. P. Phelips and E. Markham.* Second Captain and Brevet Major H. Peel Yates was appointed soon afterwards and next year Lieutenant Francis Lyon took the place of Goodenough who was promoted.

The internal economy of the Troop as it was then, may be of interest at the present time. Each set of saddlery, which consisted of black harness and blinkers, were supplied with linen covers, blue and white striped, at the expense of the subaltern officer commanding the division. This officer also supplied all the blacking and cleaning materials for his harness as the Government allowance was totally insufficient, and a monthly account was rendered to him for the extra necessary expenses incurred in making smart the division under his command. The Troop at this time was very highly thought of, and had a great reputation for drill and turn out. The discipline was, in a great measure left to the men themselves, and it was not uncommon for soldiers accused of offences derogatory to the good of the battery, to be handed over to their comrades to be dealt with. The result appears to have been satisfactory.

In 1857 Lieutenant Phelips was promoted and Lieutenant Arbuthnot† succeeded him.

One evening towards the end of July 1857, whilst the battery was playing a cricket match in a field which it had hired in Ash Vale, a mounted orderly arrived with a letter to say that "F" Troop was to march next morning to Woolwich, and prepare for embarkation to India. The Indian Mutiny was the cause. The march to Woolwich took two days. It arrived there on 24th July and after a week of strenous work, which included rocket practice on Plumstead Marshes,‡ it embarked, on July 31st at the Arsenal in the "Scotland," an auxiliary screwship,

---

* Lieutenant General Sir William Goodenough, K.C.B., and Lieutenant General Sir Edwin Markham, K.C.B. Captain Phelips retired in 1857.
† Major General H. T. Arbuthnot, C.B.
‡ A rocket carriage was part of the equipment of all Horse and Field batteries at this time.

LIEUT.-COLONEL D'AGUILAR.
(General Sir Charles D'Aguilar, G.C.B.)
who commanded the Battery in the Mutiny.

THE STORY OF "G" TROOP. 27

full rigged, but carrying 14 days coal so that steam could be used in calms.

"E" Troop Royal Horse Artillery under Captain and Brevet Major Anderson embarked at the same time in the same ship. "E" and "F" were the first two Troops of Royal Horse Artillery which had ever served in India, the Artillery in India up to the time of the Mutiny having been in the service of the East Indian Company.

After ninety-nine days voyage round the Cape, the "Scotland" arrived at Calcutta on the 7th November, and it was there decided that the Troop should form an escort for some treasure which was being sent up country. It was accordingly transhipped to one of the East India Company's steamers, the "Madras" and to a flat alongside supplied with a thatched roof and chicks. The officers were accommodated on the steamer and the non-commissioned officers and men on the flat, and so they proceeded up the Ganges, tying up every night, until on December 14th they reached Allahabad and camped below the glacis of the fort alongside the 7th Hussars.

An Indian equipment of six pounder, smooth bore guns was served out to the Battery. The horses supplied from the remount establishment were mostly young geldings, mares, and a score of old English covering stallions, fine horses to look at, but vicious and useless. After some weeks of training horses and arranging equipment the Troop was ready to move towards the end of January 1858, and on the 22nd four guns (three six pounders, and one twelve pounder howitzer) accompanied by two squadrons of the Bays under Lieutenant-Colonel d'Aguilar marched to join Brigadier General Franks' force at Secundra. This force reached Frank's bivouac at 9 p.m after a march of 28 miles, and found him expecting an attack the following morning. The troops lately arrived were weary and starving and were served out with their ration of rum before any rations had been drawn. The result was that when a night alarm occurred they were so "tired" as to be incapable of saddling up their horses. It was, however, a temporary lapse and the troops turned out only to find it had been a false alarm.

Next morning, the 23rd, General Franks attacked the fort of Secundra. Colonel d'Aguilar was in command of all the artillery and Captain Yates commanded the troop. The force marched with one Squadron of the "Bays" and Lieutenant Arbuthnot's division as advanced guard, which bore the brunt of the fighting. With the loss to the troop of one man (Bombardier Taylor) it captured the enemy's camp and two guns, and destroyed three villages in the pursuit which followed. For this work the advanced guard was specially mentioned by the general in his report.

On the 24th, advancing in the same order, the strong position of Soraon, which had been evacuated by the enemy, was taken and in the afternoon the cavalry and horse artillery returned to Allahabad. The general had no further use for them at the moment and they were required to form part of a column to march to Cawnpore. It left Allahabad on February 1st, reached Cawnpore on the 15th and a week later Lord Clyde commenced his march to Lucknow.

This city had already been twice relieved, and now some 50,000 mutineers were held at bay by Outram in his strongly entrenched position on the Alumbagh. Campbell left Cawnpore on the 24th February, and reached Lucknow on March 2nd The day after reaching Lucknow, Lieutenant Arbuthnot's division was detached together with two squadrons of the 9th Lancers and some irregular horse to join General Franks column at Selimpore, which was reached at 5.30 p.m. the same day.

Next morning Franks' detached the cavalry and the two guns of "F" together with some infantry to attack the Fort of Munshigunj. The attack was conducted by Colonel Maberly, R.A., and the Horse Artillery galloped to within 400 yards of the fort and opened fire. Then they dashed up the glacis and cleared the parapet with case shot under a hot musketry fire from the loopholes of the fort which the gunners were forced to reply to with carbines, and Lieutenant Arbuthnot himself engaged in a successful musketry duel with a chieftain in one of the embrasures.

Although the outer works were taken the keep still remained

THE STORY OF "G" TROOP.   29

intact and Sergeant Wilkins, Gunners Critchell and Dommett greatly distinguished themselves in their endeavour to blow down the gate. Lieutenant Arbuthnot was mentioned in despatches for his share in the operation. On March 5th the force returned to Lucknow and the troop was reunited and was attached to Outram's division which crossed the Goomtee at night on a bridge of boats in order to gain the northern bank. On the 7th a violent attack was made on this division but it was beaten off, and on the 19th the operations round Lucknow were brought to an end.

The rebels were routed and never again made any great stand against the British troops, but although there was no main army to fight, there were many insurgent bands still to be suppressed, and many leaders of note to be captured or destroyed.

To carry out this duty one of the operations which became necessary was what is known as the Campaign of Oude. The country in which this campaign was operated was that territory lying to the North of the Ganges between Allahabad and Cawnpore and extending northwards to the Nepaul frontier. It is divided by two rivers of note flowing from north-west to south-east, nearly parallel to the Ganges, which they join below Benares, namely the Goomtee on which is Lucknow, and the Gogra some fifty miles beyond it. Along the Nepaul frontier flows a third river, the Raptee, and it was on the banks of this, that the mutiny finally came to an end. The country is level, thickly populated and highly cultivated, and the weather which prevailed for a great part of the time, rendered the surface such as to demand the greatest exertions from men and horses.

On the 20th April Lieutenant Rideout* arrived bringing drafts from England, and took the place of Lieutenant Markham, who had been promoted second captain in the previous November, and, on the 21st May, Colonel d'Aguilar, who was in bad health, left for England on leave and Major Peel Yates assumed command of the troop.

The life under canvas in the great heat was very trying to

* The late Major General A. K. Rideout, C.B.

all ranks, and in order to keep up the spirits of the men Major Yates, who was very musical raised a troupe of glee singers in the troop who became popular not only amongst their own comrades, but amongst all the other units in the column, and served to while away the stifling evenings of the hot weather and the still more insupportable ones in the rains which soon broke.

At this time Colonel Wood commanding the Artillery forwarded the following report:—

"Some of the troops and batteries have been almost continuously on duty since leaving the camp at Buntearah and all have striven to carry on the service with the utmost energy, ability and devotion. Lieutenant Colonel d'Aguilar, C.B. . . . . Major Yates . . . . have been conspicuous from the way they managed their troops and batteries."

On the 22nd June, 1858 the troop finally marched from Lucknow at 1 a.m. with the column under Sir Hope Grant for Duneiah, with 400 irregular cavalry, part of the 7th Hussars, and the 5th Punjab Rifles where it attacked the village of Sara Gunge and drove out the enemy. It rejoined the main column at Deriabad, and next day marched on Faizabad where the left half battery assisted in driving the rebels northwards across the Gogra.

On August 9th the troop marched South with the column under Brigadier Horsford, C.B., and on the 13th reached the neighbourhood of Sultanpore. The 5th Punjabs and two guns under Lieutenant Arbuthnot were sent on towards the town, and came upon a body of mutineers, estimated at 8,000 on the opposite bank of the river. The guns trotted forward and came into action. A sharp fire was opened on them, but the shooting was wild, and the only casualty was the commander's charger. When the guns opened fire, the enemy dispersed. The depth of the water of the river prevented pursuit at the moment, but, between the 25th and 27th the troops crossed the Goomtee—the guns on rafts and the horses swimming—and captured the village of Sultanpore and encamped beside it. Five horses were

THE STORY OF "G" TROOP. 31

drowned in this day's work. The passage of the river finished up with an amusing incident which lightened the spirits of the beholders, and had reference to the officers mess of "F" Troop. Lieutenant Arbuthnot had been put in charge of this necessity of civilization, and, against all advice of those who thought they knew better, had insisted on carrying the impedimenta on camels, instead of elephants, as being so much more handy. The warning of "wait till the rains" had been unheeded and overcome, but on arrival at the swollen waters of the Goomtee the critics imagined that their forebodings would be at last acknowledged, as the camels could by no manner of means be got to face the waters. The delight of the onlookers was great then, when a string of camels, tied nose to tail, was seen swimming across the river, dragged firmly forward by a trustworthy elephant with the nose of the foremost camel affixed to his tail. For the officers of "F" Troop at any rate it was a pleasing end to a strenous day.

On September 1st, the news arived that the East Indian Company had ceased to exist, and that night the Troop drank success to India, under the government of the Crown.

Between 10th and 14th October, the Troop marched from the neighbourhood of Sultanpore to Dostpore, and on 13th the division commanded by Lieutenant Rideout, which was accompanying a detached column consisting of 7th Hussars, Madras Fusiliers and Punjab Rifles, came upon a large body of the enemy at Shakpore (Jellapur) and defeated them with great slaughter. The Troop spent the 19th at Ackbeerpore and returned to Sultanpore on the 23rd. Lieutenant Lyons division having been detached, and having taken part in an engagement on the Lucknow Road near Doadpore, captured some artillery.

The detached division rejoined at the end of the month, and on the 1st November there was a full dress parade to hear the reading of the Queen's Proclamation. "F" Troop turned out in review order—dress jackets and busbies—as if on parade on Woolwich Common, and fired a royal salute. Two days afterwards they marched under Sir Hope Grant, took Rampore Fort, on the 3rd, and on the 11th took Ameathee Fort. On this day Captain and Brevet Major the Honourable David Fraser arrived, and assumed command of the Troop in place of Colonel d'Aguilar. On the 23rd, Lieutenant Arbuthnot's division was detached with a small column under Colonel Galwey, Madras Fusiliers, and on same day attacked and captured the Fort of Rehora, and marched to the Fort of Kooli which was also captured after the guns had blown in the gates. It rejoined on the 27th November, on which date Major Fraser was engaged with the enemy at Hydergurgh on the Lucknow Road, but without decisive results. On 29th Major Fraser marched with a column under Sir William Russell and drove Beni Mahdoo across the Goomtee. This chieftain retired to the Gogra, and the headquarters of Lord Clyde's force returned to Lucknow. The Troop encamped at Hydergurgh. On the 2nd December they marched from Hydergurgh via Munshi Gange and Dilkoosha and joined the Commander-in-Chief's force at Nawab Gunge.

On the 6th they pursued the enemy to Bairam Ghat and drove him across the Gogra, having done the last eighteen miles at a rapid pace with riflemen mounted on the carriages.

On the 11th December the river was crossed near Faizabad* and the force under Sir Hope Grant proceeded in two marches to Secrora on the road to Baraitch which the force reached on the 17th and which was held by Nana Sahib and the Begum of Oude. The enemy evacuated the city, and, owing to stress of weather, Clyde stopped at Baraitch until the 22nd. He moved again on the 23rd to Intha, but heavy rain so saturated the tents that further movement was impossible, and the troops spent Christmas Day in a wet camp, and gazed at the snowy mountains of Nepal.

Next day the column was on the march again at dawn. "It was exceedingly raw and cold: a thick fog obscured the face of the country, but we could make out that it was still level and well cultivated, and the hoof and the cannon beat down rising crops of young corn."†

The village of Nahnpara was abandoned by the enemy, but after a march of 18 miles he was discovered in position with his

---

* The bridge at Bairam Ghat was not completed until the 23rd.
† Lord Clyde's despatches.

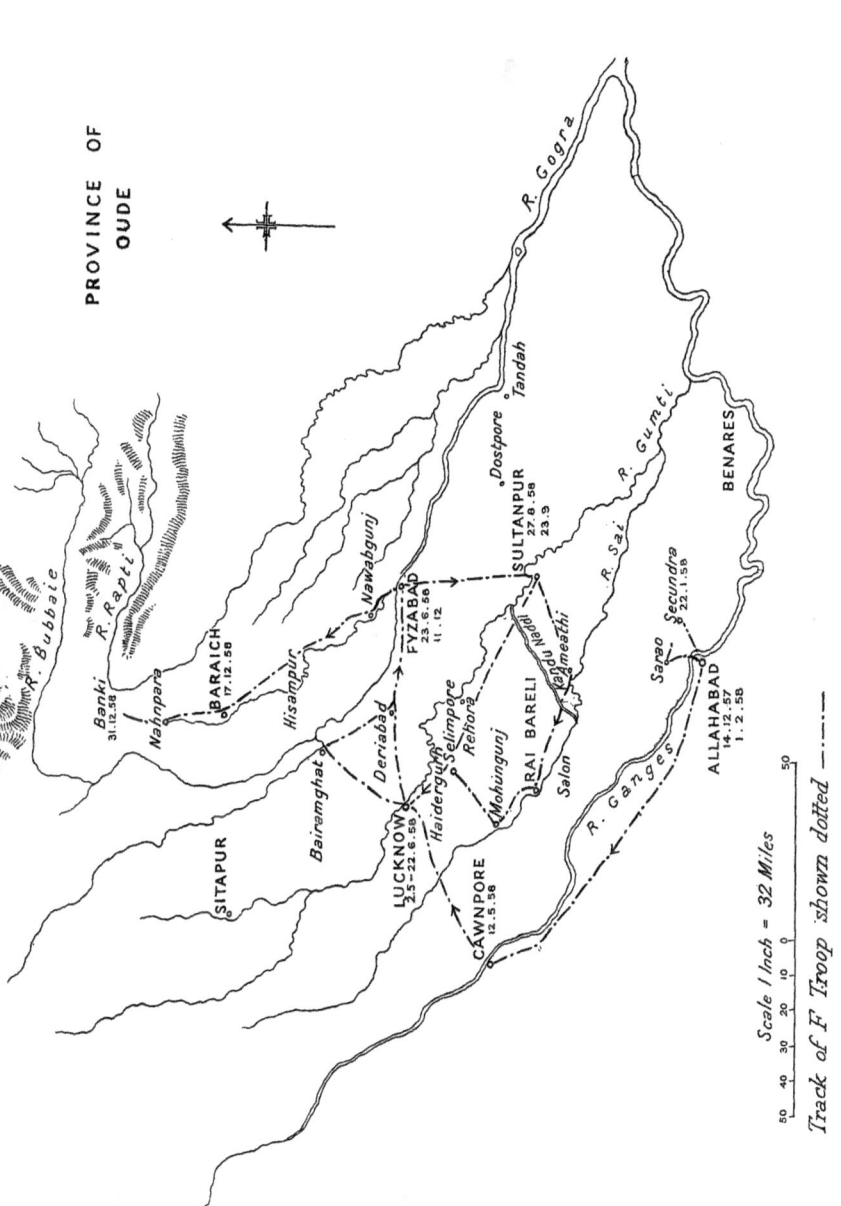

THE STORY OF "G" TROOP. 33

artillery posted among topes in the neighbourhood of Burordiah. The battle commenced at 3.45 p.m. Four guns of "F" troop Royal Horse Artillery under Lieutenants Lyon and Arbuthnot were detached to the right with the 7th Hussars, and 6th Madras Light Cavalry, and after proceeding some distance, turned the enemy's left flank when he retired. The guns followed rapidly and came into action three times The Troop captured two abandoned guns, bombarded a fort and village, and blew up a limber inside, but the enemy still fled and the pursuit was abandoned at dusk. The Nana Sahib was reported to have been with this force which lost six guns during the day. The troops were much exhausted at the end, and the Battery itself is calculated to have covered 29 miles through heavy mud. The casualties were slight.

On the next day the Fort of Meguidia was captured. The infantry attacked it in front, while "F" Troop cleared the jungle on either side. The fort which was reported to be one of the strongest of its type to be seen in India was described by Sir W. H. Russell as "a dun coloured parapet of mud, with embrasured bastions in the front of a dense forest which extended interminably on the flanks, and hid the rest of the work." The enemy fled through the jungle. Four guns were captured inside the fort, which was afterwards destroyed. The Troop then returned to Nahnpara, which it had passed through on the 26th, having lost one man killed.

On the 30th orders were received at 8 p.m to march towards Bankee where Nana Sahib and Beni Mahdoo were reported to have collected some thousand of Sepoys. It was a pitch dark night and the force was guided by the light of a lantern fixed to the howdah of an elephant. At dawn they came upon the enemy posted behind a swamp with each flank resting on a village. The guns advanced in the centre and drove him back, and then Arbuthnot's division moved up on his right flank whilst Fraser manœuvred against his left. The enemy retired into the jungle, which the Infantry cleared, and then the Cavalry and Horse Artillery drove him across the Raptee into Nepal, the cavalry following the Sepoys headlong into the river and Major Horne

D.

of the 7th Hussars and two privates were swept away by the current. Captain Stisted of the same regiment was gallantly rescued from the same fate by Major Fraser of the 7th Hussars, who, although seriously wounded, plunged into the stream and brought him to the bank. A deed for which he received the VC.

The night march on the 30th, followed as it was by a running fight all the next day, was one of the most trying pursuits of the whole mutiny. The troops were moving under arms against the enemy from 8.30 p.m. until 6.30 p.m. on the 31st, and so tired were both officers and men, that they would not rouse themselves to eat the evening meal. Fortunately their camp had arrived from Nahnpara which alleviated the distress.

They captured 6 guns, two of which were English 9 pounders and heard next morning that the Nana, the Begum and most of the enemy had fled into Nepal, and the remaining minor chiefs had surrendered. What became of the Nana is not known. He is supposed to have died during the next year, probably by violence.

So ended the campaign of Oude. The total result of this campaign included the reduction of some hundreds of forts, the capture or destruction of 150 guns, and the overthrow of forces which totalled 150,000 armed men of whom at least 35,000 were disciplined soldiers.

On the 8th January the column set out on its march to Lucknow, having on the 6th received the surrender of the Nawab of Futtighur, Mahommed Hussein, a large number of cavalry and 13 guns. Lucknow was reached on the 17th and the troop then marched on the Grand Trunk Road, via Cawnpore, and on the 18th February arrived at Meerut having covered 820 miles since the 12th November. Captain W. H. Goodenough then returned to the troop as second captain vice Yates, and during 1860 Lieutenants Arbuthnot and Rideout were promoted. The troop remained at Meerut till 12th November, 1861 when it marched to Calcutta (750 miles) which was reached on the 11th December. The centre division embarked on the "Holmesdale" transport on the 13th and 14th January, 1862, and reached Woolwich on the 28th April. The right division embarked on

THE STORY OF "G" TROOP.

the "Middleton" on the 21st January and reached Woolwich on the 12th May, and the left division embarked on the 15th January and reached Woolwich on the 24th April.

In July 1859 the Troop had been renamed "F" Battery, Horse Brigade" and it now became "F" Battery 1st Horse Brigade."

It remained at Woolwich until April 1865, when it was moved to Dublin, being then "C" Battery, B. Brigade, having been so renumbered on 1st April, 1864.

CHAPTER V.

HOME SERVICE.—THE FENIAN REBELLION.

On March 9th, 1867, the right division under Lieutenant T. B. Hamilton with cavalry and infantry marched out to Tallaght to disperse the Fenians, and next day Major Sarsfield Greene himself left by rail for Limerick Junction taking the centre division under Lieutenant Murray (the late Sir James Murray, K.C.B.). This division acted between Limerick and Tipperary and returned to Newbridge for Dublin, and in 1869 Major Greene was promoted and Captain Whinyates joined and assumed command.

The operations of the Irish insurgents did not cause any high trial to moral or fighting powers of the troops engaged against them. It was reported by the police that fifteen hundred armed men had left Dublin in the night and moved through Crumlin, and the amount of arms and equipment that was found on the roadside corroborated this statement. Lord Strathnairn, the Commander-in-Chief, in person, moved out against this force at 2 a.m. on the 8th. He took with him the Scots Greys, the 52nd Regt. and half the battery (the battery records say one section, which is probably correct). On arrival at Crumlin the General left the battery in position in advance of the church and pushed forward towards Tallaght.

The rebels were then found to be intrenching themselves on the Green Hills and the guns were sent for, but, before they arrived, either the report of their arrival, or the cold weather which prevailed, had stifled the lust for fighting in the breasts of their adversaries and the greater portion proceeded to make their way back to Dublin. On the way they attacked the police station at Crumlin, but were beaten off with loss, and the returning troops forced the remainder to give up the contest and return to their homes in search of more peaceful and safer pursuits. The troops captured 83 prisoners on that night alone and the

THE STORY OF "G" TROOP. 37

bulk of the insurgent forces was dispersed amongst the Wicklow Mountains. From the number of arms and barbaric equipment strewn along the snowy roads, one might have likened the domestic paths of County Dublin in 1867 to the tracks of Lithuania fifty-five years before. It was also an excellent example, if one were needed, of how impossible it is to make hastily raised levies compare with regular troops either in discipline, fighting powers and food supply.

The operations in the South were of somewhat longer duration, but they rapidly degenerated into a kind of partisan warfare with which the police of Corsica, Sicily and Southern Spain have grown so familar. To begin with, the well-to-do farmers of Tipperary did not welcome the insurrection at all. The weather did the rest. The country was covered with snow, and the rebels, driven from the towns by the concentration of troops, took to the wooded glens on the southern slopes of the Galtee Mountains between Mitchelstown and Cahir. Colonel McNeil, who commanded the troops in the district, easily suppressed the rising by the use of small flying columns. They did their work well in trying circumstances, but the more staid inhabitants of the district were probably right when they said that the snow had beaten the Fenians. They might have made the expression more alliterative by saying Food had beaten the Fenians, for the columns acting against them had also to endure the snow. Colonel McNeil, however, had seen to it that if his men had to endure hardships they had food and fuel to sustain them.

To sit up on the Galtee Mountains on a winter night with no food and little shelter must damp the ardour of anyone who has not the heart of a Paladin.

There were further risings in other parts of the country, which were severally brought to an ignominous conclusion, but the two mentioned were the only ones in which " G" Battery was employed.

On the 30th August the battery sailed from North Wall and disembarked at Birkenhead on the next day. From here it did a fortnight's march to Woolwich. In July, 1870, it changed station to Aldershot and received the 9-pounder M.L. Armstrong bronze guns and with them fired a test practice against a battery of 12-pounder Armstrong guns. In 1873 the equipment was again changed for 9-pounder 6-cwt. guns.

In October, 1876, being then again at Woolwich, the battery marched to Portsmouth and embarked in H.M.S. "Jumna" for Bombay and landed there on the 21st November. It reached Lucknow on the 29th, moving by rail by day and halting at night. It was subsequently quartered at Morar, Meerut and Umballa, where, on 16th July, 1888, it was refitted with 12-pounder B.L. equipment, and, on 1st August, 1889, it was renamed "G" Battery R.H.A. On the 12th October, 1889, it again embarked on the "Jumna" and landed at Portsmouth on the 6th November, whence it proceeded to Dorchester when Major Wallace assumed command in place of Major Wickham who had remained in India.

On the 20th January, 1892, together with "D" and "J" Batteries, all under Major Hunt, it marched to Windsor for the purpose of firing minute guns at the funeral of the Duke of Clarence and Avondale, and returned to its station Aldershot on completion of the duty.

MAJOR-GENERAL R. BANNATINE-ALLASON, c.b.
Commanding in South Africa, 1899 to September, 1900.

CHAPTER VI.

SOUTH AFRICA—MAGERSFONTEIN.

At the outbreak of the South African War the battery was quartered at St. John's Wood. It was included in the first orders of Mobilization and on the 29th October left its station by train for Birkenhead where it embarked on the S.S. "Pindari" of the Brocklebank Line. "P" Battery R.H.A. was also on board, and Colonel W. L Davidson, R.H.A., commanded the troops.

The ship sailed at midday on the 31st, and late on the 10th November reached St. Vincent in the Cape Verde Islands, where, as happened to so many troopships about that time, orders were received to hurry forward as fast as possible. Having disembarked the pilot, who had been obliged by stress of weather to remain on board, the ship steamed out again at 2 a.m. on the 11th, and arrived at Table Bay on the 25th, which was about the average voyage of the troopships and a week longer than the mail boats.

The officers serving at the time were Major R. Bannatine-Allason, Captain H. L. Jenkinson, Lieutenants H. W. Tudor P. de B. Radcliffe and E. C. W. Walthall.

The state showed :—

    187 N.C.O's and men.   4 A and S wagons.
    191 Horses.   1 Forge wagon.
    6 Guns.   1 Store wagon.
    6 Ammunition wagons. 1 Cart.

Between the 26th and 29th the battery rested at Maitland Camp, near Cape Town, and at 11 a.m. on the latter date entrained for the front and reached De Aar on the 1st December. It remained there, in an almost continuous dust storm, until the 7th and then trained to Klokfontein. It detrained in the early morning of the 8th and set out on the march to Modder River.

Prinsloo and Albrecht, at this time, led a thousand men down from the hills in an unsuccessful attempt to cut the railway at Enslin Station about fifteen miles down the line and made their effort whilst the battery was detraining. As firing was heard the patrols were sent out and the Commanding Officer telegraphed for permission to operate with the XII Lancers and a field battery, which passed soon after the trucks had been cleared, but permission was refused. As the road to Modder River Station was reported as being very heavy, and as some of the horses were falling sick, some draught horses were sent out from Modder Camp to help with the heavy waggons. On the 9th during a reconnaissance towards Merton's Siding the battery fired its first shell in the war.

Next day, the 10th, the battery moved out at about 2.30.p.m. in heavy rain, towards Brown's Drift and proceeded to the rising ground to the north of it. Only the firing battery and water carts were taken, the orders being that the cavalry brigade was to march to Kimberley escorting provisions. The 2nd line and baggage was to follow later.

About 2.30 p.m. the battery came under rifle fire, and took part in the much criticised bombardment of the Magersfontein position by shelling a ridge at a range of 1,500 yards and then turning its fire on to the trenches at the foot of Magersfontein Hill. When it was dark Major Allason was ordered to withdraw behind "Headquarters Hill" where the Highland Brigade was then formed up. Here the battery remained, with horses harnessed up, for several hours during which time it rained heavily.

At 12.30 a.m. on the 11th the Highland Brigade started on their forward march, and at 3 a.m. the battery followed. As the Highlanders were making their all too late deployment, a terrific outburst of fire was heard and it was supposed that the Boer position had been carried. The battery continued to advance and shortly afterwards met a few straggling Highlanders from whose incoherent answers it was gathered that something serious had happened. More accurate information was forthcoming from a Colour Serjeant of the H.L.I., and the cavalry

THE STORY OF "G" TROOP.   41

brigadier, who was close at hand, at once gave orders for "G" Battery and the 12th Lancers to advance as far as possible, supported by the M.I., and do what they could to relieve the Highlanders.

The advance had been slow for, not only was the first part carried out in darkness, but the scrub prevented rapid movement. The battery and 12th Lancers now, however, trotted forward until stopped by a wire fence. As the battery halted for gaps to be cut for the guns bullets began to whistle around, and the C.O. decided to drop the trails, and run up by hand to the top of the slope, which they were ascending, until the layers could see the enemy who were manning the next ridge about 1,400 yards away. Thus the battery took up a position which it was to occupy for thirty hours and from which, with but trifling loss, it was able to bring an effective fire on the greater portion of the Boer line. In mastering the hostile fire and preventing any further advance Major Allason obtained the able assistance of the 75th Battery of R.F.A. under Major Walter Lindsay, which had been sent up to his assistance when he had discovered that the expenditure of ammunition was likely to be heavy, to dominate the fire of the Boers and prevent any possibility of their farther advance. From this position looking towards the right front, those in the Battery could see the Highlanders lying down in rows facing the kopje which they had attacked, and beyond them, about 2,000 yards away, the Boer's trench which ran along that part of their position, and extended beyond and below the kopje. Firing over the heads of the Highlanders the Battery almost enfiladed this trench, and had also a sight of the Boer laager and the road to Kimberley. On the other flank was an almost unrestricted view of the river. Lieutenant Tudor's section at this moment knocked to pieces a Boer pom-pom, just as it had got the range of the 75th Battery. During the morning the Battery was joined by the Maxims of the 9th and 12th Lancers, "who shared with the horse gunners the credit of some of the best work done on a day of failure."* The Maxim of the former

* Major General W. F. L. Lindsay, C.B., D.S.O.
* The Times History of the War.

regiment, well placed behind a bush on the right of the Battery, did excellent work in keeping the many snipers at a respectful distance, whilst the 12th Lancers dismounted two squadrons who, under their Colonel, the late Lord Airlie, occupied the dead ground in front of the Battery where they remained, without losing a man, until midday, when they were relieved by two companies of the Scots Guards. The day was very hot and detachment gunners were working in their shirt sleeves. The supply of ammunition entailed considerable labour as the limber and wagons had to be kept under cover some distance of the right rear of the Battery, and all rounds had to be brought up by hand.

The guns although sometimes hard pressed by snipers at 600 yards or less, held on to the position which they had taken up, whilst the Brigade of Guards deployed against the Boer left. About 4 p.m. the Boer guns suddenly opened fire, but fortunately the shell burst over, and little damage was done. So they spent the evening, and the long night was passed "limbered up," practically in the firing line, with an escort of the Coldstream Guards under the late Major Henniker-Major.

Next morning, during an informal armistice the ambulances set to work to collect the wounded. Unfortunately at this moment the naval guns opened fire and the Boers replied, choosing as their target "G" Battery, which was completely exposed in the open. All ranks in the battery remained perfectly still. The drivers were mounted (some of them were discovered catching meerkats) and the Boers—it is said by the exertions of Albrecht—were soon induced to stop the fire.

About noon, on the 12th, the battery was ordered to withdraw with the cavalry in order to cover the retirement of the infantry, and, whilst coming into action about 3,000 yards in rear of the original position, the Boer guns got an accurate shrapnel range, which occasioned some casualties, including Lieutenant Tudor, who was dangerously wounded. One particular shell killed four and wounded seven horses in one sub-division, and three of the dead horses had drivers upon them who were untouched. In a few minutes the enemy's fire was silenced, and,

THE STORY OF "G" TROOP.   43

after wandering about with the Guards Brigade for about an hour the Battery returned to Camp, which was reached at 3.30 p.m. It must be considered lucky in having come through the two days with such a small loss, namely one officer and four men wounded, and a few horses killed and wounded. It had fired 1,220 shell. In addition to the Battery casualties the Brigade Major, Captain Briggs, was wounded in the hand whilst bringing in an order to the Battery and Major Maberley, R.H.A., who was acting as a brigade galloper was seriously wounded as he rode up to the line of guns to deliver a message. Excellent work was done in front of the Battery, by Lieutenant Delap, R.A.M.C., a young Irish doctor recently joined, who, regardless of the rifle fire, attended to the wounded Highlanders in the neighbourhood, and also to some Boers who were lying close by. He succeeded in bringing back many men—both friend and foe, including one Scandinavian who cursed the Boers roundly—to the line of guns, and despatching them to the rear. In recognition of the day's work he was awarded the D.S.O. It was remarkable how, after a hard day's fighting, both sides, as if by mutual consent, ceased operations, and sat and looked at one another. On the morning of the 12th one could see the Boers seated all along the line only 1,000 yards off, which in the clear South African atmosphere looked much closer, smoking their pipes and having apparently no intention of renewing the combat. These particular Boers did not apparently fire another shot, nor did they in any way interfere with the Battery retirements. Their behaviour was more like that of friends than foes. During the halt after the battle the Battery was employed in various reconnaissances up and down the river and southward along the railway line. One of these, made towards the South-East in the early part of January, lasted four days and reconnoitred the route by which Lord Roberts afterwards entered the Free State. Between the 1st and 6th February the Battery marched to Honeynest Kloof and back, but the reasons which prompted this movement did not transpire.

On December 16th Lieutenant W. L. Foster joined in place of Lieutenant Tudor, wounded. Between January 22nd, and

February 22nd the left-section was on duty on the lines of communication at Belmont. On February 8th Capt. E. C. Cameron joined vice Captain Jenkinson who had been invalided, and on this day also the battery was included in the newly formed Cavalry Division under General French, and formed, with " P" Battery R.H A. the Horse Artillery of the 2nd Cavalry Brigade (Broadwood's), the regiments being the Household Cavalry, 10th Hussars, and 12th Lancers.

CHAPTER VII.

THE RIDE TO KIMBERLEY—BLOEMFONTEIN.

On the 11th February, the Cavalry Division marched away from Modder River Camp leaving their tents standing. The battery started at 3 a.m. and advancing South East, passed Klokfontein at 5.30, and at 10.0 a.m. reached Ramdam, a farm house with a large muddy dam beside it, and here the remainder of the mounted troops from Belmont joined up. The march was resumed at 2 a.m. on the 12th but as it was impossible to keep the road, a halt was made between moonset and the first light of dawn. The Battery was to have followed the Household Cavalry, but could not do so in the dark, and having wandered about for an hour, at last formed bivouac and waited until objects became once more visible. The other units of the brigade were in a similar plight, but at dawn the march was resumed and at 6 a.m. the force came in touch with the enemy. De Wet was holding the hills to the north of Waterval Drift, and Gordon's brigade, with the assistance of the fire of "O" and "R" Batteries turned him out of this position. French, with the remainder of the division, galloped for De Kiel's Drift which was successfully crossed, and a counter attack which the Boers made against the right flank, ended in failure. "G" Battery was only slightly engaged on the right, and the bulk of the fighting fell to the other battery of the brigade. The battery bivouacked on the right bank of the river without baggage or rations, for the transport had been blocked by that of Tucker's division and the scene on the other side of the drift represented a confused mass of waggons, yelling drivers, and mule teams tied into knots. The efforts of regimental officers to bring forward the baggage and supplies of their own units ended in failure, and the battery obtained no food or forage until nightfall.

Next day (the 13th) in spite of the hurry to press on, the start was late owing to the consequent failure of supplies, so it was 9.30 a.m. before the battery moved off. The horses had been watered early and were left to cross the arid and often burning wastes between the Riet and the Modder in a boiling sun without water. The march for the right of the division, with which the battery was, was made longer owing to French's feint towards the north-east to deceive the Boer commando which was threatening his right flank. The battery finally reached Klip Drift on the much longed for river, with its running water and banks fringed with green trees, at 6.30 p.m. Possession was gained after a small but sharp fight. On this day's march 18 horses out of the battery alone dropped down from exhaustion and were left upon the veldt, and many others were suffering from concussion and were unfit for work.

Next day the Cavalry Division remained at Klip Drift whilst the infantry moved slowly but steadily onwards and occupied the positions in rear. The Boers opened a long range gun fire which was somewhat annoying but not in the least destructive. On this day the Battery received a considerable number of horses from the Ammunition Column, which remained practically immobile, and about sixty battery horses were left behind for the sake of rest. Most of these rejoined after Paardeburg. One section was on outpost duty all this day, and food for men and horses was very scarce.

15TH FEBRUARY.—KLIP DRIFT.

Cronje having at last divined the true significance of French's move had despatched Froneman and de Beer, with Albrecht and two guns, in all about 800 men to stop it. These commanders took up a position on a semicircle of hills north of the point where the Modder River makes a bend between Klip Drift and Klip Kraal Drift. The road to Kimberley ran through this position over a shallow nek. The Boer left covered the main laager and Magersfontein; the right, the road to Blomfontein. The Boer generals evidently expected the well known dismounted frontal attack, but instead for the first time, they were to experience the charge of well handled cavalry. For

THE STORY OF "G" TROOP.   47

French decided to break through. Gordon's brigade had advanced up the river from Rondeval Drift and his guns ("O" and "R" Batteries) advanced into the plain and opened fire on the eastern kopjies. Shortly afterwards the batteries of the 1st Brigade (Q, T and U) galloped on to the ridge behind them and opened on Albrecht's guns. Albrecht however had already been firing on this ridge and had got the range to a nicety so that he was able to pour a destructive fire on to this brigade before the batteries had marked the exact position of his own guns. So destructive was the fire that "G" and "P" Batteries were ordered forward in support, but before they got there the cavalry formed up and charged and the order was cancelled.

Gordon led the charge with the 9th and 16th Lancers. He was followed by French himself with Broadwood's brigade and "G" and "P" Batteries followed it with "T" "Q" and "U" a little behind.

The fight at Klip Drift has been much commented on in recent years. Its main incident has been used by British and foreign writers as an example of cavalry tactics, as a demonstration of the necessity of the *arme blanche* and as an argument for its discontinuance. It is unnecessary in this work to discuss these reasonings, but one must mention two items which appeal to the regimental officer and which, though being human and instantly absorbing, are ignored in the scientific discussion of tactics. One was the rapid decision of the general in command and the equally rapid manner in which his orders were carried out, the other was the spectacular display, which raised the enthusiasm of the onlooker in a way which no slow moving attack of infantry could have done.

To those who stood in the plain and watched the squadrons gallop past, the day will for ever be a day of memory, and it is no exaggeration to say that those few minutes on that February morning did more to raise the spirits of the troops than the actual relief of Kimberley itself.

One can picture the scene even now after many years. The low rough line of kopjes in front, shooting out spits of flame, where the rifles found a dark background, and which raised around us little spurts of dust, like worm casts, where the rifle bullets struck the sandy ground. On our left rear were Albrechts guns, hurling their shell on to the ridge behind us, on which Rochfort's brigade had just appeared. And from the hasty glances that we were able to throw in that direction it seemed to be a line of smoke, and flying sand and dust.

Then, on our right, in the opening of the hills which led towards the Modder, appeared a line of horsemen, indistinct and quivering, as figures in a mirage. Suddenly the line seemed to surge onwards and fling itself into the valley like a wave which breaks and spreads itself along a sandy beach.

The gun fire ceased. The fire from the kopjes seemed to cease also, and in front of us, headed by one or two horsemen passed a line of cavalry, themselves fully visible, but churning up a cloud of dust that partially hid the lines in rear. We saw them, however, indistinctly, line after line clouded in dust, and after them the guns. We likened it afterwards to a gallop past in the Long Valley on a hot summer day. But this was real. The Long Valley—our utmost soldiering until then—seemed so far away and so counterfeit. For this was war: the other a mockery.

The division rallied at Abonsdam, and the battery then passed on with Broadwood's brigade westwards towards Alexandersfontein, which lies south-west of Kimberley. The garrison had captured it on the previous day, and the Boers were engaged in an attempt to retake it when the appearance of Broadwood's brigade put an end to their desire. The battery went into bivouac about 8 p.m. near Benaauwheid.* Next day, the 16th, for the battery was a day of rest, but by the evening the news of Cronje's movements had come through and, at midnight, orders were sent to all the available troops at Kimberley to prepare for another effort. On the 17th the Battery and "P" Battery marched off at 2.30 a.m. with the rest of the brigade. The cavalry regiments were very weak and their baggage was

---

* The actual position of the Battery was at a farm known as Benaauwdenhoutsfontein. The second brigade was acting as a stop between Cronje and Kimberley.

THE STORY OF "G" TROOP. 49

left behind. About 8 o'clock it halted for a short time, and, at about 11.30, it reached Kameelfontein, a spot on the direct line to Koodoosrand Drift, which French had decided was the most likely spot for Cronje to cross the Modder, and here the force surprised a Boer outpost having breakfast at a farm, and also captured most of the Boer signallers and their equipment. At the same time a line of waggons was reported advancing up the north bank of the Modder, and just as the Battery horses were being watered the guns were hurried forward to a low ridge about 1,500 yards North of the drift at Wolvekraal where the enemy were about to form laager. "G" and "P" Batteries then opened fire and were answered by two or three Krupp guns which were soon silenced. The Boers then made an effort to seize a kopje which lay about 1,000 yards on the right flank; the 10th Hussars followed by "G" Battery raced for this point and forestalled them. The position was held throughout the afternoon, and even after dark the battery continued firing one shell every ten or fifteen minutes into the laager. Although the Boers had made a determined attempt to storm the kopje, and the fighting was at close range, the casualties were slight. That evening the M.I. were sighted about four miles off moving up the river bank, and one knew that the infantry must be close, and that the reign of Cronje was nearing its end.

The cannonade was continued on the next day, and after some time, in order to co-operate with the infantry who were now surrounding the laager, the Battery moved forward to closer range. The Field Artillery now began to arrive on the scene and the horse batteries, tired out with thirty-six hours of continual marching and fighting, withdrew to Kameelfontein, where the units of the cavalry brigade assembled for food and rest. On the 19th, "G" and "P" Batteries and the 10th Hussars on account of supplies crossed the river at Paardeburg Drift and bivouacked there. They were afterwards joined by the rest of the brigade which next day reconnoitred the Boer position at Kitchener's Kopje.

On the 21st February the battery took part in the action

E.

for the recapture of Kitchener's kopje, the hill lying to the east of the laager which had been retaken by De Wet, and on the 23rd it was moved with the rest of the cavalry division to the other side of Koodoosrand Drift. On this day Lieutenant Delap, R.A.M.C., who had endeared himself to all ranks by his untiring devotion, succumbed to enteric fever and was removed to hospital. From this date until the 1st March one section was detached on outpost duty with the Household Cavalry, and during this time, on 27th, Cronje surrendered. It was the first great triumph of the British Army during the war, and the success was especially a moment of rejoicing to "G" Troop, which had fired the first shells which forced the Boer train to halt in its tracks. After three days of intense wet and short rations, the Cavalry Division, on the night of the 6th, was ordered to move to Osfontein a few miles south-east of Koosdoosrand Drift, preparatory to turning the southern flank of the position which the Boer generals had taken up on an S shaped ridge of hills, stretching from Poplar Grove on the Modder River, and ending in a line of kopjes known as the Seven Sisters. This position barred the road to Bloemfontein. The force left Osfontein at 3 a.m. on 7th March and passed round the southern flank of the Boer position whilst the infantry moved up to attack the front. At about 6 a.m. gun fire was opened from the Boer position upon the Division. The latter moved out of range and eventually found itself on the left rear of the Boer position. Shortly afterwards General French having advanced found the Boers leaving their position and sent back for all his Horse Artillery which thus got separated from their brigades. Porter, advancing without his Horse Artillery, "G" Battery, who had also got separated from "P" and its brigade, attached itself to the 1st Brigade and opened on the Boers retreating across the open towards the North and East. Little damage was apparently done.

Some time afterwards when the Cavalry turning movement on the right had been successful the battery joined up with the other Horse Artillery batteries, which advanced in line under Colonel Davidson, and shelled the Boers' final position on

THE STORY OF "G" TROOP. 51

Slagkraal Hill. The effect appeared to be small, but it induced the enemy to evacuate his positions and retire across the Modder River. On this day the Battery was estimated to have covered thirty miles through deep sand between 3 a.m. and 7 p.m. There were no casualties among the men, but two horses were shot dead, and six more died of exhaustion. Seeing that the remainder had been fed on totally inadequate rations for many days before, it is indeed wonderful that they should have lasted through the day as they did, and the failure to make the battle of Poplar Grove the success which was intended, must be attributed not to the plans of the generals, or to the willingness of the troops, but to the impotence of the horses to carry out the required movements.

The battery bivouacked that night near the farm of Poplar Grove, so named from a grove of poplar trees which grew beside it, and foraged for food, both for man and beast.

Next day the brigade which, had been obliged to bivouac some six miles away to the north-east, was reassembled at Poplar Grove and some rations were collected. Lieutenant Foster went sick, and Lieutenant Tudor, having recovered from his wound, rejoined.

On the 10th the division advanced once more in three columns towards Bloemfontein. The 2nd brigade took the centre road and by 8 a.m. the Battery came into action against the Boers who were holding the Driefontein position. In the early afternoon they reached the Boers left flank and fired against the southern extremity of the Bosch Rand Ridge but were not allowed to press forward, which was a disappointment to all ranks, who felt that had the brigade advanced much damage could have been inflicted on a demoralised enemy. As it was the Boers made good their retreat, and the battery bivouacked on their position at 7 p.m. with very little food for men or horses, and, but for the timely arrival of a stray herd of frightened sheep, and the green crops which surrounded the position of the guns, it is quite possible they might have had nothing at all. Next day they advanced in the rear brigade, and bivouacked after a ten mile march; and, on the following day, they did 34 miles in 14½ hours, reached the railway six miles south of Bloemfontein where they bivouacked at John Steyn's farm and captured him. The railway was blown up in the afternoon. On this day 14 horses were placed hors de combat from exhaustion. Although fighting was going on in front and on the left no enemy was sighted by the battery, although as it grew dark the flashes of their pom-poms became visible.

On March 13th the Battery moved off, the 2nd Brigade leading, and came in sight of Bloemfontein at 5.30 a.m. Advancing north-east of the town the Battery halted about half a mile from it and the men were supplied with whisky and bread by the grateful inhabitants. The Battery bivouacked that night at Saltzmans Farm, Bloemspruit and the first portion of the war came to an end.

CHAPTER VIII.

JOHANNESBURG AND DIAMOND HILL.

A fortnight later, on the 28th, at 2 p.m. the Battery was ordered out to Glen on the Modder River and marched at 4 p.m. Appalling confusion was caused by the infantry columns which blocked all the drifts, and, after vain endeavour to get through in the dark, the Battery, and "P" Battery, bivouacked at 10 p.m.

The reason for this move was that the Boers had concentrated on the hills overlooking Karree Siding, about 13 miles north of Bloemfontein on the Brandfort road, and Lord Roberts had decided to dislodge them. Some of the cavalry units crossed the Modder River that night, and at early dawn on the 29th the whole division was across and proceeded to make a wide turning movement to the west, whilst General Tucker's division attacked the Boer position in front.

In the afternoon the Battery was in action facing eastwards towards Houdenbek Hill and was replied to by three or four Krupp guns. The Boers retired in safety along the railway and the Battery returned to Glen in the dark, having been on the move from 5.30 a.m. to 8.30 p.m. Next day it returned to Bloemspruit. The fight at Karree Siding was an indecisive action, but the terrain on which the Cavalry acted was much cut up by drains and wire fences which rendered the movements of mounted troops especially difficult, and the information concerning the enemy's movements does not appear to have been sufficiently clear to enable the Cavalry to cut off the enemy's retreat from the position he had taken up. Either this or faulty co-operation with the infantry was probably the cause of the division being halted for some hours in the morning and thereby giving the Boers the opportunity to escape.

On the 31st at about 6 a.m. heavy firing was heard from

the east and about 2.30 p.m., the Battery moved off in that direction and halted at Springfield Farm, where they met the remnants of General Broadwood's brigade returning from the fight at Sannahs Post.* It marched at dawn next day and reached Koornspruit at 10 a.m. and found the Boers lining the rising ground beyond the stream. The Battery came into action against the Boer Artillery whilst Broadwood's wounded were gathered and the dead buried. General retirement was then ordered, but the Battery received no order and was left out with a troop of the 9th Lancers, and, when they finally withdrew, a local Boer guide missed his way, and conducted them to Waterval Drift on the Modder, where they passed the night. Next morning they joined the main force at Bosman's Kop, and later in the day retired to Springfield. The Battery returned to Bloemspruit on 3rd where it remained until the end of April.†

During April the Battery was almost entirely rehorsed. One hundred and fifty-three horses and ten ponies joined, also one hundred and twelve mules, but most of these were shortly afterwards removed. Casualties amongst the men were also replaced so that the time at Bloemspruit was fully occupied in training horses, fitting harness and generally getting ready for the next move.

On May 1st the battery joined General Hutton's division of mounted Infantry, which made a long march across the Modder River at Glen, reached Brakpan on the 2nd, and on the 3rd turned the Boer right flank on the hills north-west of Brandfort. The battery shelled the Boers who subjected it to some hot rifle fire, but eventually retired and Tucker's division entered the town.

On May 2nd four horsed maxims joined the Mounted Infantry and were attached to the Battery. They did useful work upon several occasions.

On the 4th, Hutton advanced on the left of the main columns in order to cross the Vet River and cut the railway at

---

* It is noteworthy that the G. and P. were originally ordered out with Broadwood and T, Q, and U were ordered to make them up with horses. Colonel Rochfort, however, objected, so two of his batteries were sent instead.

† The Major was absent from these operations as the result of an accident at Karree Siding.

THE STORY OF "G" TROOP. 55

the junction at Smalldeel. He found De la Rey strongly posted on a long ridge south of the river near a place called Constantia. "G"Battery came into action against this ridge whilst Alderson's Mounted Infantry turned the enemy's right flank. The Boers retired to the Vet River, but Hutton did not consider himself strong enough to pursue his advantage.

Following on this, on May 5th, the Battery supported the attack of the New Zealanders on Mistquasfontein Drift five miles west of the railway. Supported by Alderson, the action was successful and that night the Battery spent on the north bank of the Vet. Two days later, the cavalry having now arrived, there was a reconnaisance towards the Zand River, when the Battery and New Zealanders were attacked by the Z.A.R.P., assisted by a heavy and effective shell fire but the attack was repulsed with some loss. Here the Battery came in sight of the main Boer force, assembling on the railway line, just north of the river. The last train was seen to start for the north, and then the line was blown up. On May 9th they crossed the Zand River at Duprees Laager, and pushed on towards Kroonstadt, which, after some severe skirmishing on the 10th and 11th, was reached on the 12th. The Battery halted until May 19th during which time it received fifty-six horses and ponies.

On the 20th, marching at 7.30. a.m., the cavalry division passed along the Klerksdrop road, and on the 23rd reached Parys and next day at 3 p.m. struck the Vaal at Viljoen's Drift. Porter's brigade crossed on that day, they were the first troops to enter the Transvaal, and the day was the Queen's birthday.

The advance continued for the next three days and on the 27th French was engaged near Olifants Vlei.

About 10 a.m. on the 28th the scouts drew fire and shortly afterwards several Krupps and pom-poms opened fire upon the column. "G" Battery galloped forward to within 2,500 yards, whilst the cavalry threatened the Boer right flank and after an hour forced these guns to change position. They then pushed on and came into action near Van Wyks Rust, some distance to the right of "O" Battery in an exposed position on a low bare hill, which gave no shelter from the rifle fire, which, as well as an ineffective gun fire, appeared to be coming from all points of the compass. In the dusk General French, who saw that the movement could not succeed, withdrew the cavalry south of the Klip River in order to await the arrival of the supporting infantry, but Hutton's Mounted Infantry with "G" Battery remained all night where they were, covering the Cavalry. On the 29th, still under cover of the Mounted Infantry and the Battery, the retirement was continued in the direction of Doornkop where the Boer right flank had been located. In the fighting which occurred this day, Quarter-Master Sergeant Havern lost his right arm. He was carrying a bucket of water between two gun teams, which were halted at a few yards' interval, and which had just been watered, when a shell struck him and shattered his right wrist. It did not burst, and no one else was hit. Lieutenant Delap, who had rejoined, remained behind and amputated the arm below the elbow.

These two nights had been very cold. The water was all turned to ice, and in the morning the ground was white. The rank and file suffered severely, and the fact that the last manœuvres had not been understood by them had a somewhat depressing effect on the junior ranks. General French of course had to withdraw and move westward leaving his place to be taken by the infantry under Hamilton—a flank march performed not without confusion.

The Battery bivouacked that night near the position where Dr. Jameson had surrendered three years before, and on the following day continued their turning movement round the northwest of Johannesburg. Near Driefontein, they came upon some of the enemy outspanned, and after some fighting the Mounted Infantry captured a long range Austrian Skoda-Pilsen gun with a limber, which had been captured at Colenso from the 66th Battery, Royal Field Artillery, and ten wagon loads of ammunition. The detachments had been put to flight by the Horse Artillery fire. About seventy prisoners were also taken. The force bivouacked that night near Klipfontein, and on the next day, 31st May, Johannesburg surrendered.

THE STORY OF "G" TROOP.   57

On the 1st and 2nd June the Battery bivouacked ten miles out of Johannesburg on the Pretoria road. On the 3rd it marched off at 7 a.m. in rear of the 2nd Cavalry brigade. In the early afternoon General French came upon the enemy posted amongst the rocky kopjes west of the Crocodile River and sent forward flanking parties to drive them back. The Boers, who ultimately proved to be part of Du Toit's commando from Fourteen Streams, developed an unexpectedly severe fire and first two guns of "G" were ordered up and then the whole Battery in support of the Cavalry, whilst the Mounted Infantry commenced a flanking movement. The enemy then withdrew and the troops biouacked at Kalkheuvel, after a long and trying march over a very hilly country. Next day, June 4th, they marched at dawn, but the road was so blocked by wagons that only eight miles were covered by the Battery, which bivouacked on the Crocodile River. On the 5th the Battery marched with Hutton eastwords along the Pretoria-Rustenburg Road, whilst the cavalry passed through Commando Nek and marched parallel to him, but north of the Magaliesberg Range, in order to relieve the prisoners at Waterval. That night was spent four miles out of Pretoria and the town surrendered.

On the 8th the Battery marched to Deerdepoort with the force destined to take part in the northern of the two turning movements designed to force De La Rey and Botha from the extended position which they had occupied covering the Middelburg district and the railway to Koomati Poort. The next two days were spent without movement whilst Louis Botha repaired to Pretoria to treat for peace. At this time Lieutenant J. E. C. Livingstone-Learmonth joined the battery for duty. At the conclusion of the futile negotiations Lord Roberts decided to carry out his turning movements, to drive the Boers eastwards and take possession of the positions about Elands River Station in their rear. To accomplish this French was to move northeast via Kameelfontein to Doornkraal and drop southwards to the railway at Witfontein. His force consisted of 1,590 men and 12 guns ("G" "O" and "T" batteries) and the enemy opposed to him was estimated at 4,000. Added to this the British flanks were twenty miles apart.

On the 11th June French advanced into the valley of the Pienaar's River, and advanced to Kameelfontein Drift at the foot of the ridge of the same name. On entering the valley which lies beyond the river the troops were fired on from three sides and especially from the Bockenhout's Kloof Ridge. Dickson assisted by "T" Battery captured the kopje, known as Loubaken Hill, above the drift, whilst "O" Battery advanced into the valley and suffered severely. Then the Boers under Snyman commenced to creep along the Bockenhout's Kloof Ridge to the north, and Porter's brigade was sent to forestall them and frustrate their attempted turning movement towards that flank. "G" Battery followed with Hutton and dropped into action on a low ridge near Roodeplaats Farm where General French had taken up his position. This was an excellent supporting position. Practically the whole field could be seen from it, and Major Allason was able to successively to assist Porter, "O" Battery, and Alderson's Mounted Infantry. About 4 p.m. the Battery was moved forward in support of "O" Battery which, having got into a rather nasty position, was suffering heavily. "G" incurred some casualties among the horses, but none amongst the men. This state of affairs lasted till dusk when the battery bivouacked in the centre of the valley. So ended the first day of the Battle of Diamond Hill.

During the night the Boers shifted the position of several of their guns in order to command the Kameelfontein drift and to enfilade the cavalry positions, and a piece of heavy artillery which had been in action near Edendale in the right centre of the enemy's line had been moved more towards the right. Its services in the centre were apparently not required and the enemy was concentrating his attention on trying to get between French and Pretoria. This artillery opened fire against the positions of Dickson and Alderson on Loubaken Hill, as well as on the drift and the country beyond and caused considerable annoyance. The General ordered Major Bannatine Allason to stop this fire, so he withdrew his battery across the river by a

THE STORY OF "G" TROOP. 59

very indifferent drift behind Roodeplaats, and, escorted by the New Zealanders, brought it into action against two fifteen pounders. Although the battery had been brought into action "under cover," the fire was at once replied to by five or six guns of various calibre stationed in different places including a 40 pr. firing Melinite. The Battery was literally plastered with mud and stones but none of the shell burst. This engagement lasted until dusk, when the Battery withdrew to its original position, having put out of action the only two guns within range—the fifteen pounders—and killed or wounded all the detachments including the German commander. So heavy had the Boer fire appeared to French that he sent Hutton to see if the Battery could carry on. General Hutton was astounded to find that not a man or horse had been hit and called out "Thank God, good old G's all right." The absence of casualties was indeed astonishing as the Battery had drawn the whole Boer fire for about four hours, and so greatly relieved the rest of the line.

There was no firing during the morning of tne 13th and about noon it was discovered that the Boers had vacated their positions during the night. The cavalry had lost touch, which accounted for the lateness of the information. At 1 p.m. the Battery advanced up the valley, and crossing the mountains by the Crocodile Spruit Pass, reached Doorn Kraal at 8 p.m. Some Boer waggons and ambulances were seen retiring in a north-easterly direction. The operations of Lord Roberts and Ian Hamilton against the centre on the previous day had been followed by the withdrawal of the whole of the hostile right flank. Next day, the battery returned to Deerdepoort where it remained until the 23rd. On the 18th, Waterloo Day, the battery gave a sort of dinner and "sing-song" which was attended by many friends including New Zealanders and Canadians.

CHAPTER IX.

THE ADVANCE EASTWARDS.

The Boers, driven back from Diamond Hill, had, during the enforced delay in Lord Roberts' operations, collected in the mountain districts round Pretoria especially to the south-east between the Delagoa Bay railway and Springs (east of Johannesburg where a depôt had been formed) ready to pounce upon any weak spots in the line of defence and on parties guarding the railway. Several raids were carried out, and finally General Hutton with a mixed force was sent south-east to clear up the situation.

His foremost troops under Pilcher consisting of 400 M.I. and "G" Battery set out on June 23rd, and marched to Riet Vlei, but one section of the battery under Walthall was almost immediately detached to Boshkop Farm, two miles north of Zwavel Poort where it remained until July 4th when it rejoined headquarters. On July 5th Hutton concentrated his force at Rietfontein. His main objective was a Boer force reported to be twenty miles south-east and threatening the railway line to Johannesburg, so next day he sent Mahon with 1,000 men and "M" Battery down the Standerton Road.* In the early hours of a bitterly cold morning Mahon was attacked by about 300 Boers which after a sharp fight he defeated. He then returned to Rietfontein. On the next day Mahon was engaged in the direction of Bronkhurst Spruit against the Boer forces holding the Tygerpoort-Witpoort ridge. In the afternoon the battery was sent to his assistance which enabled him to withdraw from a somewhat strained position.

* On the 6th the R.A. of this force consisted of G and M batteries R.H.A., 66th battery R.F.A., 2 guns R.G.A. (5 inch), 6 pom-poms, 3 sections A.C. The whole commanded by Major Bannatine Allason.

THE STORY OF "G" TROOP. 61

Next day the enemy, evidently much reinforced, again pressed the attack and placed himself astride the roads to Middelburg and Standerton. It was necessary to check this movement and the Mounted Infantry and New Zealanders were thrown out to do so. The Battery accompanied them. It was in action during the whole of the day and was at intervals subjected to a heavy shell fire, which, however, was not effective. The following day was a repetition except that the fighting took place more in the direction of Koffy Spruit.

On this latter day French, with Porter's brigade from Kameelfontein, began to move to Hutton's assistance, and, on the afternoon of the 10th, he reached Riet Vlei. The general, with the object of keeping the enemy concentrated so that he might be defeated in a pitched battle later on, decided to turn both flanks and dislodge the opposing forces without dispersing them. On the 11th therefore Porter moved round the southern flank by Leeuwpoort. Hutton, with the M.I. and "G" Battery advanced directly on the Witpoort ridge. Alderson, Mahon and Pilcher operated on the north. The Boers were turned off the ridge but the movement could not be carried through to its logical conclusion, for the Boers were found to be massing to the north of Pretoria, and this fact, together with the news of the disaster of Zilikats Nek made the reinforcements of the Pretoria garrison imperative. The mounted troops returned to their bivouacs, and French, taking Mahon's and Pilcher's commands, returned to Pretoria. The Boers promptly reappeared near Witpoort Ridge, where a party of Irish Fusiliers had been left on guard.

From the 12th to the 15th the battery remained quietly at Riet Vlei, but, on the 16th, the Boers under Ben Viljoen made a desperate attempt to recapture the Witpoort Ridge and cut off Hutton from Pretoria. The outpost line along the ridge was attacked at dawn and the guns were ordered forward up the line of the Koffy Spruit. The battery trotted on under a heavy shell and rifle fire to within 1,500 yards of the ridge and there took up its position, and later on Lieutenant Walthall's section was detached to support Major Munn, who, with four companies of the Irish Fusiliers, forty New Zealanders, some Canadians and two pom-poms, was holding a detached post on the ridge against about six hundred Boers. The advance of this section was a risky operation. Walthall, however, succeeded in getting his guns into action within about one hundred yards of the enemy and opened fire. The effect was electrical and from that moment the infantry got the upper hand.* The post had been gallantly held throughout most of the day in spite of two strong attacks by Viljoen and Pienaar, which attacks did not cease until Alderson was able to take the offensive on our left and threaten the enemy's rear. By sunset the enemy had retired from the ridge. On the 20th, Walthall's section was sent to join French in order to replace a section of "O" Battery which had been destroyed at Zilikat's Nek.

On the 23rd, the situation round Pretoria having been cleared up, French commenced his advance to Middelburg with the object of severing the enemy's communications with the Eastern Transvaal. Gordon moved on the right, Dickson in the centre, whilst Hutton with the M.I. and "G" Battery passed in a north westerly direction over the Witpoort Ridge, and then, turning south-east, crossed Koffy Spruit and Bronkhurst Spruit and arrived at Boschpoort near the Wilge River. The battery exchanged a few shots with the enemy just before sunset, but no fighting of importance took place.

On the 24th, Hutton advanced slowly with many Boers ahead. At 1.30 p.m. the battery trotted forward and crowned a ridge looking towards Vlakfontein. The enemy retired but his movement was covered by a veldt fire under cover of which he was able to bring into position a pom-pom and Krupp gun which engaged the battery for some time. The bivouac that night was at Vlakfontein and next day the column pushed on towards Groenfontein, near Balmoral coal mines. A good deal of anxiety was caused on this night owing to the disappearance of the Brigadier who had gone out towards the coal mines to

---

* Just before the arrival of the section the Canadians, in order to relieve the situation, made a gallant charge in which they lost two officers and several men. They were buried in the dark when operations had ceased.

THE STORY OF "G" TROOP.   63

have a look round, lost his way in the dark and only managed to struggle back to the bivouac in the early dawn.

Meanwhile Gordon and Dickson (with whom was Walthall's section) had driven the enemy before them up to Olifants River where he was reported to be bent on making a stand. French determined to turn them viâ Naauwpoort, and Gordon with the 14th Hussars and Walthall's section moved on there on the 25th. After a half hearted defence by the enemy he made himself master of the drift and passed to the east bank. At this time a terrific thunderstorm burst over the scene. The rain came down in sheets and the slopes of the drifts became almost impassible for guns. The Boers had made good their retreat and pursuit was out of the question so the troops went into bivouac in heavy rain which when it ceased gave place to an icy wind that was almost worse than the wet.

At 6 a.m. on the 26th the Battery marched for Olifants River which it reached after a trek lasting for two hours. The drift was a bad one at any time and the recent rain had made it almost impracticable for carriages. The crossing therefore entailed great delay upon the battery and by the time the guns were across it was too late to render any assistance to the cavalry, who were skirmishing to the south-east in the direction of Sterkwater. Hutton spent the night at Good Hope Farm on a tributary of the Olifants River and at 10 a.m. next day, 27th, he entered Middelburg, a pretty little town with a good water supply and surrounded by luxurious vegetation.

The change and prospective rest was welcomed by the troops, but they did not then foresee that they were to remain in the neighbourhood long enough to grow exceedingly weary both of the place and its environs. For from now until the end of the year the battery was employed in the outpost scheme of occupation, and the days were spent in small movements in the vicinity and that mostly in sections. Doornkop, Bankfontein, Pan, Wonderfontein were all in turn occupied, evacuated and returned to by the various sections, nor was there any fighting to enliven the movements, which soon showed signs of becoming monotonous.

On the 3rd September, Major H. F. Mercer, the grand nephew of the hero of Waterloo, arrived at the battery headquarters in Middelburg and took over command from Major Bannatine Allason who was about to be promoted. The battery was at this time distributed as follows: Headquarters, Middelburg; Lieutenant Buchanan at Wonderfontein; Lieutenant Livingstone-Learmonth at Bankfontein; Lieutenant Walthall at Pan. This last section varied the monotony of the time by being seriously engaged on the 6th, in support of the post of Nooitgedacht which had been strongly attacked.

On the 11th, the battery was once more concentrated at Middelburg, and on the next day the news was received of the flight of President Kruger to Delagoa Bay. A few months earlier his flight might have caused depression to his friends and exultation to his foes, but now even the men recognised that his presence was an encumbrance to the forces in this guerilla warfare, and his name would be as useful in Europe as in the Transvaal. So the battery remained at Middelburg and prepared for further efforts.

On the 21st, Mercer made a two days reconnaissance of the country lying to the north, but without gaining much information. On the 25th, Lieutenant E. F. Calthrop joined from the R.F.A. in place of Lieut. Livingstone-Learmonth who was promoted.

On 15th October, another reconnaissance towards Klipfontein produced some mild fighting, and next day the Chestnut Troop arrived from the east by train, and exchanged equipment with "G". "G" Battery gave up the 12 pounders, and men eligible for service in India, and in exchange took 15 pounders and reservists. The two batteries spent a cheery evening together over a camp fire, and next day the Chestnut Troop left for Pretoria and home.

On the 19th, Lieutenant J D. B. Fulton took the place of Lieutenant Buchanan, and Captain E. H. T. Parsons succeeded Captain Cameron who had been ordered home on promotion.

At this time Major-General the Hon. N. Lyttelton made Middelburg his headquarters and Colonel E. M. Flint, Royal

BRIGADIER-GENERAL H. F. MERCER, C.B.
Commanding in South Africa from September 1900, to the end of the war.

THE STORY OF "G" TROOP. 65

Field Artillery, assumed the duties of station commandant and C.R.A. Lines of Communications. The troops stationed there at the time were the 18th Hussars, 21st, and 85th Batteries, R.F.A., 1st battalion of the 60th Rifles, the Dublin Fusiliers, Leicester Regiment and D.C.L.I.

Then followed a quiet fortnight except for one unsatisfactory brush with some Boers, and the time was spent in preparing for further moves and in holding a miniature army championship of cricket and football.

It was at this time there took place the movement that is known as the Boer revival. Following on the departure of Kruger and the cutting of the communications with Delagoa Bay the Boer resistance had seemed broken. Many burghers had taken the oath of neutrality, a greater number had quietly returned to their farms, the last resistance in the Free State lacked a head, and the South African Government and leaders of the Transvaal were collected in the north in the Pietersburg district. In August came the awakening in the Free State which was galvanised into life by the arrival of De Wet. Following on this, the Transvaal also rose, and the leaders at Pietersburg broke up to head the various risings. Of these, Ben Viljoen was given orders to take command of the north-east, to re-organise the commandos, and assume the offensive. On November 19th, he arranged simultaneous attacks on Balmoral and the Wilge River, the first of which he conducted himself and entrusted the other to his lieutenant, Müller. At 7 p.m. on that day the Battery received orders to entrain for Balmoral. They did so with four guns, and reached Balmoral at 9 a.m. only to find that Viljoen's attack had failed, and that they were too late to be of much assistance. Viljoen then took up a position near Rhenosterkop. The last order issued by Lord Roberts before his departure deputed to Paget and Lyttelton the task of driving him from this position. Paget attacked him on he 29th, but through misunderstanding the co-operation was faulty. On the previous day four guns of the Battery had set out with a small force under Col. Payne for Doornkop, but Payne's orders were insufficient,

F.

and little was effected. For three days the force skirmished round Doornkop and Lammerkop, and, on the 1st December, in pouring rain, returned to Middelburg, having marched fifty miles and fired 120 rounds.

A week later the Battery took part in a similar movement under Colonel Campbell, K.R.R., and moved viâ Olifants River to Watervaal Drift. This time the force got in touch with Paget and operated on his left flank in the country known as Hell. They returned to Middleburg on the 11th. Two more small expeditions were undertaken during the month, but otherwise the time passed quietly until the beginning of the year. Christmas was spent at Middelburg with as much gaiety as possible, which meant that the tents were decorated with bush scrub, and plum puddings were supplied.

At this time Lieutenant Walthall was promoted, and his section was temporarily commanded by Captain Parsons.

So ended the year 1900.

CHAPTER X.

SOUTH AFRICA, 1901.

The events detailed in the last chapter described the part played by the Battery in the Transvaal outbreak at the close of the year 1900. The awakening of the States was succeeded in the ensuing year by a more aggressive policy on the part of the guerilla commanders.

Unrest in Cape Colony and success of their arms in the Transvaal and Free State had raised before them the idea of an invasion into their enemy's country. De Wet himself was as usual the leader, but his first essay was without success. Two raids, however, succeeded in a greater measure and induced a reorganisation of the British forces, in the conquered territories. The first of these, under Commandant Herzog, crossed the Orange River near Colesburg, cut the railway north of De Aar, and then, moving viâ Britstown and Prieska, turned south to Calvinia, and in time actually reached the sea at Lambert's Bay, and threatened the territories of Beaufort West, until driven back by the operations of De Lisle.

The other under Kritzinger crossed the border at Rhenoster Hoek and pushed on towards Burghersdorp. From there, engaging the pursuing columns in several skirmishes, it moved viâ Steynesburg to the neighbourhood of Middelburg, and eventually penetrated as far as Aberdeen and Willowmore in the heart of Cape Colony.

These isolated raids were not of great importance in themselves, but they gave valuable information to the South African government in showing how hostile forces could penetrate to the heart of the British occupation without suffering loss.

Acting on the information thus obtained, De Wet, now recovered from the defeat of a first attempt at invasion, passed the British posts between Thabanchu and Ladybrand and penetrated as far south as Dewetsdorp. This movement had been foreseen by Lord Kitchener, who, in the early part of the month, had reorganised the forces at his disposal. In accordance with these orders, on the 7th January, "G" Battery was withdrawn by train from Middelburg to Pretoria. In order to avoid horse sickness which was then prevalent, the Battery was accommodated in the Staats Artillery Barracks, but the remedy was worse than the disease, as in a few days the horses developed glanders which eventually forced them to move into camp once more, and to undergo a process of inoculation, as a result of which twelve of the best immediately died. The Artillery Barracks had many shortcomings, but the brief sojourn in them was a relief to those who had spent fifteen months on the veldt. The stalls, although small, were fit for Leicestershire hunters, and the quarters were fitted with electric light and bath rooms, which can only be appreciated by those who for many a long day had performed their ablutions in the open air, in a perished india-rubber tub, or in the same receptacle in a leaky tent by the light of a guttering candle.

One of the operations decided on by Lord Kitchener was a big move into the eastern Transvaal, and " G" Battery was ordered to supply two guns for this operation. On the 24th January, Lieutenant Calthrop's section moved out to join Alderson's force in order to take part in this movement.

On the 28th, Captain Parsons left the Battery to act as Staff Officer to Colonel Jeffreys, who was in command of some M.I., and on the 30th, the order was received to stand ready to proceed to Cape Colony in order to frustrate the projected invasion of De Wet.

On February 6th, the Battery marched to the station to entrain, but found nothing ready. No trucks were available until 8 p.m. and it was not until after midnight that the Battery was fully entrained and ready to start. A long and heavy train eventually moved out at 4 a.m. on the 7th. It was divided into two portions, irrespective of the position of the trucks conveying men, horses or carriages, and and the officers were finally crowded together in one of the guards' vans. The train reached

THE STORY OF "G" TROOP.   69

Bloemfontein at 9 a.m., arrived at Norvals Pont at 7.30 p.m. on the 9th, and finally reached Naaupoort at 4 a.m. on Sunday, 10th, where the Battery detrained and went into camp. It now formed a portion of Colonel Bethune's brigade, which was to consist of the King's Dragoon Guards, 3rd Dragoon Guards, Prince of Wales's Light Horse, " G" Battery, R.H.A., and one pom-pom under Captain Connolly, and of this force Major Butcher, R.F.A., was brigade major. It was one of the columns collected under the charge of General Lyttelton, who had been removed from the eastern Transvaal to take charge of these operations.

De Wet, on entering the Colony, had moved westwards, and, inaccurate information as to his actual whereabouts led to a good many orders and counter orders in the circumventing columns. Eventually, on the 12th, the Battery entrained for Hanover Road, where, in the midst of a severe dust-storm, which of course turned to rain, they detrained on a siding without any platforms. A cold and cloudy morning ushered in a soaking wet day. The camp was knee deep in water, horses standing up to their hocks in mud, bivouacs were blown down and every discomfort which nature could devise visited the hapless column. It is but fair to say, however, that Plumer's troops who were actually on the march, in pursuit of De Wet during those days, suffered still more severely from the terrific rain, yet succeeded in capturing some ammunition waggons and prisoners.

On the 15th, the weather cleared, and the Battery entrained for Richmond Road, where the 3rd Dragoon Guards, fresh from England, joined the force. There followed a night disturbed by loose horses and false alarms. Several animals of the various regiments got mixed up, and the Battery records mention that horses that had been neither born nor intended for draught turned out excellent in their new position.

At 4 a.m. the brigade moved towards Britstown and joined General Bruce Hamilton's force at a place called Barnard's Dam where it spent another wet night. The following night—also wet—was spent at Britstown itself. It moved at 5.30 a.m. next day, 19th, in pouring rain, and for the first time came in touch with the enemy, but the Battery did no shooting. That night they bivouacked at Houwater. It was on this day that De Wet reached the Orange River and found himself for the second time in three months stopped by the flood. He therefore decided to abandon his enterprise and retire back to his own country.

The change in De Wet's movements occasioned some alterations in the pursuing columns, and, on the next day, after some counter orders, the Battery moved slowly forward at 8.30 a.m. It halted for some hours in the middle of the day, and again at night, and eventually, on the morning of the 21st, reached Beer Vlei. A similar forced march on the next two days brought the Battery to Kleinbrach Kuil and back again, and, on Sunday the 24th, they had a much needed rest. On the previous day Plumer's weary troops, after a forced march, had again struck into De Wet's rearguard, and on the Sunday that chieftain, once more doubling in front of his pursuers, had crossed the railway line between Kraankuil and Orange River Station, actually passing his men by single file through the pickets of the New Zealanders who had come out from Kimberley with a force to block his way. On the 26th, Bethune's Brigade moved to Hopetown, and in the evening pursued its way to Orange River Station, where they rested in a very congested bivouac, and where many troops from other columns had joined up, all under orders to entrain at once. Hurry, however, was now unnecessary, for, on the 28th, De Wet had found a drift—Botha's Drift near the Colesburg Bridge—the fifteenth he had tried in nine days, by which his men could cross over. With great relief the commando, which now included Hertzog's men, gladly passed out of the colony which a short while before he had been almost as pleased to enter.

It cannot be claimed for the Battery that they had taken any great part in what has since become known as the Great De Wet Hunt, but, by means of long marches and the utmost exertion of both men and horses, they had the satisfaction of knowing that they had helped to foil this dangerous irruption into Cape Colony.

THE STORY OF "G" TROOP. 71

On March 1st, they crossed the Orange River and followed on the track of the guerilla chief in the direction of Fauresmith, and on Sunday, 3rd, were brought up sharp by a terrific storm, which was so bad that it put an end to all movement, and the Battery spent that night at Tituspan near Luckhoff. From Fauresmith it turned north with Plumer's column, on the 7th, reached Pietrusburg, and next day, for the second time in the campaign, arrived at Abraham's Kraal. Then, moving by Aasvogelkop, it reached Bloemfontein on the 10th. The last three days had been spent in heavy rain and the camp at Bloemfontein was two feet deep in mud. Both men and horses were worn out, and suffered severely from the shocking state of the bivouacs.

De Wet meanwhile had reached Senekal, close to where he had started on the 26th of January, when he broke up his command. The great De Wet hunt had come to an end. He had marched at least 800 miles, and the pursuing columns had covered nearly as much ground.

The romance of this phase of the campaign was undoubtedly furnished by the Boer leader, who had entered his enemy's country, and for two and a half months had overcome the difficulties created by pursuing columns, swollen rivers and terrible weather, and finally, having disturbed the whole scheme of British occupation, had escaped to the country from which he had come. The success, however, must be accorded to the British Commander-in-Chief and to the Generals who had put their forces in motion in his pursuit. De Wet's invasion soon ceased to become an invasion, and degenerated into the wiles of a hunted fox. The pursuit may be likened to the manœuvres of several well managed packs of hounds all acting in concert. If De Wet's manœuvre was meant as an invasion pure and simple, it was a failure; if it was to draw away troops which should have been acting against Botha it was also a failure. And, clever and resourceful as he had shown himself, he had left the colony with a loss of several hundred men, all his guns and baggage, and, what for him was worse than either, a loss of prestige. When De Wet crossed the Orange River, the chance of a Boer rising in Cape Colony came to an end.

During the halt at Bloemfontein Captain Charles Stirling joined the Battery in place of Captain Parsons, and the time was spent in refitting the Battery and replacing as many as possible of those horses which were unfit for further work.

On the 14th, the Battery once more set out upon its road to take part in the first of the "drives," which from now onwards were to become the main feature of the campaign. Lieutenant Fox's section went with the 3rd Dragoon Guards towards Kaffir River, and the remainder of the Battery, with the 7th Dragoon Guards, marched eastwards, passing across Koorn Spruit through Sannah's Post, and the Waterworks, a march of great interest to all ranks on account of the mishap of the preceding year which they had been just too late to avert. On the 19th, the centre section rejoined at Ramahatjes and the march was resumed during the next three days, in drenching rain, through Shanz Kraal, Hout Nek, to Welgevonden. At Shanz Kraal they were joined by a section of "O" Battery, and during their marches the column collected enormous herds of sheep and oxen which had to be driven along very slowly, and made the movements both tedious and dull. The columns then crossed the drifts over the Vet and the Klein Vet Rivers, heavy slopes and rivers swollen with rain, and in the evening of Sunday, 24th, they pitched their bivouac, in a dreadful downpour, to the north of the little town of Winburg. Here the column got rid of the sheep and cattle and received orders to join General Elliot's division at Kroonstadt.

On the 27th they set out for this place, moving almost due north through Ventersburg. The Battery was engaged on the 28th, in clearing the Boers from Zand River Drift, whilst the right column—the force was marching in four columns—cleared the ridges of the Doornberg, the original stronghold of De Wet. At Ventersburg the force got rid of new collections of cattle, whilst the outposts prevented the Boers from interfering with the operation, and then moved viâ Geneva siding and Bosch Rand to Kroonstadt, which was reached on April 2nd.

THE STORY OF "G" TROOP. 73

Here General Locke-Elliot's division was formed. It consisted of the Brigades of Bethune, Broadwood and De Lisle. Here also the Commanding Officer received the first news of the right section since leaving Pretoria, which was then reported at Utrecht. The headquarters of the column were as follows:

Major-General Locke-Elliot, C.B., D.S.O., Commanding.
Major Hoare, 4th Hussars, C.S.O.
Captain Pitman, 11th Hussars, D.A.A.G.
Captain Lloyd, 21st Lancers, A.D.C.
Captain Ashburner, 7th Fusiliers, A.D.C.
Captain Smyth, 21st Lancers, Intelligence Officer.

A portion of this force consisted of seasoned warriors who had been fighting for many months, but added to them were certain novices such as the Prince of Wales's Light Horse (a new South African corps) and three battalions of yeomanry fresh out from England, whose knowledge of warfare had been obtained from books or legends. The regular troops were the K.D.G's (581), 3rd D.G's (317), 7th D.G's (580), I.Y. (1,000), South Australians (326) and portions of 62nd and 82nd Batteries, R.F.A.

The next two days were spent in inspections by the General Officer Commanding and by the C.R.A. (Colonel E. M. Flint, R.H.A.) who both expressed pleasure at the state of the Battery and especially at the condition of the horses.

On the 10th, the weather changed from being wet and became fine and very cold, and the column marched off in the direction of Rhenoster River which was reached on the 13th. Three days later it approached the Vaal at Shoeman's Drift, and, turning eastwards, traversed the difficult pass of Rhenoster Poort, from which place one section of the Battery was ordered forward to take part in an engagement between two portions of our own force. The mistake was happily discovered before any damage was done.

On the 17th, the Battery reached Parys, a township which the Boers proclaim to be the gem of South Africa, and which, with indifference to orthography, was named after the capital of

France. The next day was spent in collecting not only the sheep and oxen, but also the whole of the men, women and children from the village, who were forthwith marched *en masse* to Vredepoort Road on the main railway line, where they were got rid of, and here also the commanding officers were able to get money from Kroonstadt to disburse to the men their long overdue pay, and provisions to replenish the scanty supply of their messes. It must be noted that about this time, owing to the cold winds and dry atmosphere, the grasses of the veldt began to dry up, and the horses were therefore deprived of the nourishment which they had obtained from grazing during the halts. They still grazed, it is true, but the result was far from satisfying, and soon began to make a noticeable difference in their condition.

On 26th April, Heilbron was reached, and from there a small force with one section of the battery was sent off to collect some Boer guns reported to be buried in the neighbourhood. The search, however, proved futile. The next day they marched off again in pursuit of some wagons. Having shelled a farm, and driven out some Boers, the K.D.G's went in pursuit of the wagons, and captured one of them, but they also captured 2000 sheep, 200 oxen and 200 horses. The force camped that night at Vechtkop near the monument of the battle field where in days gone by a few Boer men and women had withstood the attacks of Mosilikatze's hordes. The night was very cold, it had rained all the afternoon, and between one and three a.m. a heavy thunderstorm raged, which drowned the previously frozen bivouac.

The force moved on next day in the direction of Frankfort. The marches were slow, and some desultory fighting took place. They crossed the Wilge River, and, on 7th May, reached Villiersdorp, cleared the Boers out of some holdings on the far side of the river, and moved eastwards. The column then advanced along the south bank of the Vaal, and, on the 11th, reached its tributary, the Klip, at Driekuil Drift. Next day they marched to Delange's Drift, and halted there until the 15th. The force then followed up the Klip River as far as the Commando

THE STORY OF "G" TROOP.

Spruit, and then crossed the ridges to the Klip River once more, when they had some sharp engagements with various parties of Boers. Finally they arrived at Botha's Pass, and obtained a view over the mountains of Natal.

Having encircled the range known as the Witte Kopjes and cleared the Boers out from the neighbourhood, the G.O.C. went on with De Lisle to Harrismith and the remainder of the column returned to Delange's Drift, which they reached on May 28th, having had a few brushes with the enemy en route.

On 29th, the Battery crossed the drift, and marching in the teeth of a gale of wind which was blowing over the burnt veldt, they reached Standerton, where the columns of Plumer, Knox and Bruce Hamilton were already collected. The thirst produced by wind and dusty veldt was providentially quenched by a deluge of rain, which greeted the troops as they moved into their bivouacs.

That the above-mentioned commanders, who were supposed to be operating more or less separately in different districts, should have found themselves gathered together in one small area leads to the conclusion that the attempted subjugation of the Free State by district commands had not turned out a success. Elliot was now ordered to lead his division back to Kroonstadt viâ Reitz and Lindley, and the force started on June 3rd, when the rearguard consisting of the 3rd D.G's and a section of "O" Battery got rather roughly handled by a force of Boers who arrived from no one knows where, and " G" Battery was in action for some time in support of them. Advancing through Leeuwkop on the 5th, the column reached the Wilge River, and the General heard that a Boer convoy was crossing his front some fifteen miles to the westward. He at once sent forward a small force to intercept this, and the operation was successful, but the prize was not very valuable, consisting, as it did, chiefly of a womens' laager of 120 wagons and the accompanying escort. These were parked in the farm of Graspan near Reitz.

At this time Steyn, De Wet and De la Rey, with their respective bodyguards, were on their way to meet the Transvaal commanders, and had halted for the night within five miles of the place where this episode occurred. They immediately decided to retake this column, and attacked the place where the waggons were parked, forcing the defenders to retire to a Kaffir kraal. The Battery was hurried forward in support of these troops which had originally captured the convoy. It was hotly engaged for some time with the Boers across the river, and then forcing its way across a very bad drift, one section went forward and cleared the remaining Boers from the kraals and kopjes. It camped that night at Stridjpoort. On the 7th, the force arrived at Lindley, a day of confusion, as Lowe's column cut across Bethune and the baggage was inextricably mixed. Next day, the 10th, Lieutenant Calthrop's section rejoined the Battery after an interval of five months, and on the 13th the column once more reached Kroonstadt.

This section had left Pretoria on the 25th January, to join Alderson's Column which was to take part in the movements conducted by French to sweep up the Boers in the eastern Transvaal. The column consisted of Alderson's own Mounted Infantry, the Yorkshire Light Infantry, "J" Battery, one section of "G" and a pom-pom. It was concentrated at Mooiplaats, 10 miles east of Pretoria, and other columns under Eustace Knox, Pulteney, Allenby and Dartnell stretched southwards prolonging the line of advance to Springs. This line started in a south easterly direction on the 27th, sweeping the Boers before it, and devastating the country. On the 3rd February, being joined by the columns of Smith-Dorrien and Campbell on the north, it was formed in a semicircle, the imaginary chord of which stretched from Carolina nearly to Standerton. The scheme had, however, partly failed, for Beyers and Kemp had already escaped and the main part of the Boers, attended by baggage, women and children, were trekking hastily eastwards towards Swaziland.

On February 6th, the forces were concentrated in a circle round Ermelo, and Botha attacked the northern wing (Smith-Dorrien) at Lake Chrissie where he was defeated. The force extended again and moved eastwards, pressin before them the Boers who fought rearguard actions almost daily. Alderson

THE STORY OF "G" TROOP. 77

having passed to the north of Ermelo, marched south-east, and on the 15th February was at Derby, twenty miles south of Amsterdam. He then moved to Piet Retief and joined in the operations against the enemy in the country lying between Natal and Zululand. On March 31st, the section of "G" Battery was at Smaaldeal, and on 6th April, at Vreiheid. It then entered Natal. On April 16th, it was at Dundee and then returned to Newcastle and, on 29th April, left by train for Kroonstadt.

During these operations the hardships endured by the troops were severe. The scheme of supply had broken down and French had great difficulty in feeding his forces, which were weakened by withdrawals for the operations in Cape Colony.

Heavy rains were the order of the day, which made the country so bad that it seriously interfered with wheeled transport and made the drifts impossible for supply columns. Yet the drive was not without result, for although the chief Boer leaders had managed to escape, they had lost over 300 killed, about 1,000 by capture or surrender, 11 guns and vast quantities of vehicles, horses, mules, cattle and ammunition. It had one other effect which was perhaps more important, and that was stopping Botha's projected raid into Natal.

Lieutenant Calthrop's section remained in and round Kroonstadt until the beginning of June, when, as previously stated, it rejoined the rest of the Battery.

On the 17th June, the Battery was inspected by Lord Kitchener and Sir William Knox, who both complimented it on the excellent work which it had done during the recent drives, and next day Waterloo Day was celebrated by as good a dinner as could be obtained, which chiefly consisted of potatoes, bread and beer, and this was followed by a camp fire and sing-song, and an issue of rum.

The Free State commanders, who, up to the present had fared somewhat luckily in the guerilla warfare, were now to suffer a severe shock, and the Battery was part of the force which had the great pleasure of bringing this event to pass.

Elliot, once more refitted, commenced to sweep for the second time over the north eastern district. He moved in four columns, Broadwood, Bethune, Lowe and De Lisle, and left on June 22nd, Bethune with the Battery being on the left. The column swept the country in a south easterly direction between the Zand and Valsh Rivers, and after daily skirmishes, on the 28th, they struck the Lindley-Bethlehem road, and there crossed the Valsh, when rumours began to fly about of the movements of hostile convoys, and of the presence of Boer Generals in the immediate neighbourhood. From here also they got into helio communication with Harrismith. The columns here turned northwards and moved on the Wilge River.

On the 6th July, De Lisle's column moving through Reitz found a document proving that the Boers were in the habit of leaving the place when the British columns approached and returning to it when they had passed; therefore on the 10th, when the Battery itself was as far north as the Frankfort-Heilbron Road, the General swung back his right (Broadwood) and sent it by a forced march into the town of Reitz. He galloped into the town at daylight, and found there Steyn with his bodyguard, General A. P. Cronje, Generals Wessels and Steyn (brother of the President), and captured the whole of them except the man they wanted to capture most, namely Steyn, who escaped practically naked on a pony. He left, however, £11,500 in Free State notes behind him. Unfortunately De Wet had not slept in the town that night.

After this haul, Broadwood rejoined and the column made a left wheel. The Battery marched into Heilbron on the 13th, and having detached a section to De Lisle who came up on the right, marched forward and reached the railway at Komeboog Spruit. As it had been arranged that the Battery would reach the railway at Grootvlei, and stores, etc., had been sent to that place, the change of march resulted in great confusion.

The result of this drive was that the columns had killed and wounded seventeen Boers and captured sixty-one. They had also captured 7,000 horses, 7,000 cattle, 6,000 cartridges and 300 waggons.

Colonel Bethune left the column for a short while and

THE STORY OF "G" TROOP.

Colonel Lowe took his place as commandant. The column moved on again on the 15th, and marching viâ Ventersbloom and Plessis Rust, crossed the Rhenoster River at Wildebosch, then followed round the bend of the river to the colliery at Vierfontein, a bad march, long and uninteresting, the last day of which, the 23rd, was over a sandy waterless desert.

Next day the march was continued over burnt veldt, to Coal drift on the Vaal amidst decaying sheep and oxen, which had been slaughtered by a previous column, and the Battery halted at Nooitgedacht, three miles from Klerksdorp.

It spent four days here, and during this time Lieutenant Delap rejoined. Then the column turned upon its tracks and proceeded to take part in Elliot's big drive in the north of the Free State. It crossed the Valsh on the 31st, and captured some wagons and prisoners, and on August 3rd, in the neighbourhood of Bulfontein, they captured a Boer laager, consisting of 70 waggons and carts, and 1,000 head of cattle. On the same day Broadwood and Owen made a similar capture. The forces joined up at Reitpan. The Battery had been sixteen hours on the march, and had done about 45 miles. For the next few days the column marched southwards verging on Glen. Sections were sent out at intervals in search of wagons, etc., and many of these, as well as horses and cattle, were collected. Finally, on the 14th, the whole force reached Glen, and hastily refitted, which was more necessary than usual now as several horses had been poisoned by eating tulip grass. Whilst at Glen, Lieutenant Fulton's section rejoined from De Lisle's column, and Lieutenant Fox's section took its place. At the same time Lieutenant Calthrop left to go in charge of a pom-pom section, and Lieutenant Hawkesley was appointed to the Battery.

Elliot's column having concluded this last drive was now, with practically no rest, sent up on another, against the commands of Haasbroek and Froneman. The idea being to form a line between the railway at Glen and the Basuto border at Ladybrand, and drove the enemy north-east over the Wittebergen into the Brandwater basin where other columns were posted to receive them. Following on this idea, the Battery left Glen on August 18th, and next day crossed the railway line beyond Karee Siding and marched in a north-easterly direction to the Tabaksberg, and, leaving Winberg on the left, moved on to Wittebergen. De Wet and Haasbroek were reported in front, but beyond daily skirmishes with small parties of Boers, their commandos (if they were there at all) were not greatly in evidence. What was more trying to the column than the enemy was the nightly deluge of rain and the cold winds which succeeded. The rains were endured with fortitude because they brought forward the young grass on the veldt, but the winds were condemned by all as being neither good for man nor beast.

The column manoeuvred round Wittebergen for some days, basing itself upon Witkop, and then turned on its tracks in the direction of Winberg, the neighbourhood of which was reached on September 5th. Here Lieutenant E. W. M. Cuninghame joined from the 63rd Battery, R.F.A. and Lieutenant Fox, who was nearing promotion, was ordered off to command a pom-pom depôt. The column then circled back over its old trail of months before, and passing by Witkop, crossed the Senekal Road, encircled the Biddulphsberg and reached Bethlehem on the 22nd. Next day it marched out towards Harrismith and bivouacked at Elands River, where orders were received to entrain for Ladysmith.

To understand what follows, one must now hark back some weeks to the doings of Botha in the Transvaal. The approach of spring had brought new life to the veldt, and also to the men who lived upon it, and the various commandos sprung into life as in that season a young man's fancy is supposed to turn to love. Botha had collected a force near Ermelo, and, with the prospect of gathering strength as he advanced, he determined on a second invasion into Natal. He therefore struck down at the frontier south of Utrecht and defeated a mounted force under Gough at Blood River Poort. The various columns, however, had now been put in motion, and Botha found it impossible to enter Natal from his present position; he therefore turned south towards Zululand, but was held up by

THE STORY OF "G" TROOP.

small British posts at Fort Itala and Fort Prospect. The failure of his attacks on these posts where, for his modest force, he had lost a considerable number of men, induced Botha to relinquish all idea of invasion. He therefore retired in the direction of Vryheid.

The news of Gough's fight reached the Battery on 26th September, and on the 30th, Bethune's column entrained at Harrismith, and on the 1st October a portion of it reached Durban. The railway arrangements appear to have been very indifferent, and for one or two days amorphous portions of the Battery were scattered over the Natal railway. In fact, one truck which included the Sergeant-Major and several men and horses, did not reach Durban until the 4th. The remainder of the Battery had already passed through the town and reached Stanger about fifty miles up the coast, near the mouth of the Tugela River where they spent some days in inactivity—a most welcome inaction—as it allowed the horses to fill their bellies with good grass, and the men to get a much needed breath of sea air.

At 4 a.m. on the 5th, the brigade marched along the coast and at 10.30 the Battery crossed the Tugela River. The wagons of the Imperial Yeomanry, however, stuck in the drift and eventually had to be ferried across, which delayed the whole column. This, as far as it concerned "G" Battery, was somewhat of a blessing, as it permitted the Sergeant-Major and his belated party to rejoin. On the 7th, the column reached Eshowe, where they spent a very wet and windy night, and where General Dartnell's column joined them. It was at this time that news of Botha's retreat reached the column, and they received orders to return to Durban. On the 15th, they once more reached Stanger, and then followed an outbreak of coast fever, which reduced many men to a state of absolute incompetence. The idea was that the brigade should march to Ladysmith via Greytown, but the health of the men absolutely prevented this idea, and after several contradictory orders regarding the entraining and marching of the transport and of the brigade, which

G.

necessitated the baggage column performing an unnecessary march, it marched into Durban on the 26th, and entrained there. It reached Maritzberg at 11 p.m., Ladysmith 9 a.m. 27th, and Harrismith 3 p.m. on the same day, where it went into quarantine at Nels Farm. News was received here of the blowing out of the breech of a gun of the centre section, and the consequent deaths of Sergeant Scott and Corporal Whitcroft at Goedelegen on the 21st, and on the 29th the Sergeant-Major was removed to hospital.

The weather at this time was very trying, the sun during the day was hot, but it clouded up at night and the evening was ushered in by heavy rain-storms. When these cleared off they were replaced by bitter winds which had a terrible effect on both men and horses. A storm on the night of the 30th, was described as a "perfect blizzard" and the atmosphere on the succeeding nights was little better.

In the beginning of November there were fourteen columns placed round the circumference of the north eastern Free State, and on the 6th, orders were issued for the whole of them to march upon Paardehoek, an isolated group of hills about 25 miles south of Frankfort, with the object of encircling the Boer columns who were known to be within the district. The drive, however, was generally a failure as the Boers got news of the movements and escaped between the columns. They lost about 100 men, but they also lost 10,000 cattle and 200 wagons. The Battery marched up the Wilge from Harrismith, and on the 11th crossed Bezuidenhout's Drift, where it became apparent that there was nothing of importance within the enclosing circle. The Battery then returned to Harrismith which it reached on the 15th. The column then moved towards Bethlehem.

Meanwhile the Free State commanders had again been in consultation regarding the course of the war, and on the 13th November, De Wet and Steyn had met at Bligdschap to discuss a letter from Botha concerning terms of surrender. They rejected these terms and prepared themselves for fresh enterprises. On the 28th they called a council of war, which was interrupted

THE STORY OF "G" TROOP. 83

by the news of Elliot's move from Harrismith. He was sweeping north-westwards by Bethlehem and Lindley towards Kroonstadt. Elliot, however, was ignorant of this concentration of Boer commanders, and the Battery records merely report that De Wet was supposed to be in the vicinity with one gun and two pom-poms.

It was Rimington who really got full information about this concentration, and who engaged the enemy at Spytfontein, but he was unable to effect much, and finally withdrew from the action. De Wet then moved to Lindley, and on Sunday, 1st December, the Battery once more reached the neighbourhood of Kroonstadt. On the 3rd, Lieutenant Cuninghame's section was sent to join De Lisle's column which was also at Kroonstadt, and Lieutenant Hawkesley joined Broadwood. On the same day Lieutenant Fulton* had a fall and broke his collarbone. The Battery then worked its way along the Lindley blockhouse line to Doornkop. The blockhouse system had been inaugurated some weeks before, and, as far as the north east Free State was concerned, was completed in January, 1902.

On the 7th Major Stirling rejoined from Lowe's column which had been broken up.

On the 21st December the Battery became complete again and marched with the K.D.G's, 7th D.G's and 6th M.I. under Colonel de Lisle who had taken command, temporarily, of General Broadwood's column. On the 22nd they reached Quaggafontein overlooking Lindley where they spent Christmas Day and luckily were able to obtain all the Christmas gifts sent out from home, as well as plum puddings and beer for the men. Sports were arranged during the afternoon, and were interrupted by a severe storm in the evening. Meanwhile De Wet had scored a great success at Tweefontein, and was marching off with his booty, leaving Prinsloo in command of his troops. De Lisle got close to his rearguard on the 27th, and had a skirmish with the force beyond Fanny's Home Drift. The enemy took up a position on the Stabbertswaag, covering a

---
* This officer rejoined at Doornkloof on December 14th.

drift in front of them, and whilst the Battery took up a position opposite to them, Lieutenant Cuninghame's section moved on to the next ridge under the fire of some guns and pom-poms, and succeeded in knocking out one of the latter. Darkness came on and ended the combat, which with another hour of daylight might have been made decisive for the British force. It is noteworthy, however, for the fact that it was the last time that a commando of Free State Boers in any force faced a British column in the field. The Battery covered thirty-three miles that day. It left its bivouac at 4.30 a.m. and retired into another at 9 p.m.

Prinsloo slipped away in the night and the pursuit was continued at dawn the next morning, but on the 30th, all trace of the enemy was lost.

So ended the year 1901.

CHAPTER XI.

THE END OF THE WAR.

The commencement of the year 1902 synchronised with the commencement of the new phase in the warfare, namely, the new system of drives. The old system where columns had pursued an elusive enemy for days and nights had resulted in much wear and tear of men and horses without any successful conclusion to their efforts. Now, however, that the blockhouse lines were completed, the columns were able to hold their enemy in a ring fence, when the chances of their escape were reduced to a minimum. Another change of moment was carried out, namely, the conversion of the Artillery into Mounted Rifles. As far as "G" Battery was concerned, this change took place at Kroonstadt on the 20th and 21st January. After two days of rifle practice the Battery entrained for Heilbron, and on the 28th marched along the blockhouse line to Brakvlei and next day to Frankfort, where six Horse Artillery Batteries were all camped together, namely, G, O, T, P, J, and R, under Colonel J. L. Keir. G and R Batteries formed one group under Major Mercer, together with two guns of the 5th battery and one pom-pom.

In the beginning of February the Artillery Rifles held the blockhouse lines towards Heilbron, whilst the other columns drove up to them. The result was about 280 Boers captured, but De Wet, who was in the prescribed area, managed to break out to the south and crossed the blockhouse line between Kroonstadt and Lindley. This drive ended up near the railway junction of Hoek, and, on Sunday the 9th, the Artillery Mounted Rifles marched back to Heilbron to prepare for the second drive. For this drive the columns wheeled about and extended from the Heilbron-Frankfurt blockhouse line across the Vaal to the

Natal railway. The Royal Artillery Mounted Rifles extended as stops from Heilbron to Frankfort, which place was reached on the 17th. On the 20th they extended to Tafelkop, and next day they marched in the drive, with their right on the Wilge, and their left in touch with Damant. On this day Rimington cleared the Bothasberg, and there was a lot of firing as the Boers in desperation were trying to break through. Elliot, Lawley, etc., who had been driving south of the Kroonstadt Lindley blockhouse line, had come up on the Wilge, and now acted as stops on the Right of the Royal Artillery. De Wet who with Steyn had returned into the eastern Free State, found himself now with two or three commandos, hordes of cattle, waggons and women in the centre of the approaching drive. The drive was at this time holding Hol Spruit which flows from the Natal mountains in a westerly direction and joins the Wilge south of Strydpoort. On the night of the 23rd De Wet himself with part of his force broke through the line between Rimington and Garratt, whose commands were not strong enough to be able to hold the line of the winding river. Most of the Boers, however, recoiled southwards, and on 25th, they held the line of the Cornell's Spruit, whilst Elliot on the Right was now able to strengthen the contracted line on the Wilge, over which one or two small commandos had managed to escape. On the 27th the force made the biggest capture that the British troops had carried out for over a year, namely, the whole of Meyer's commando, 571 strong, which were surrounded a few miles north of Harrismith. The total result of the drive was, 50 killed, 10 wounded, 759 prisoners, 25,000 head of cattle, 200 waggons and carts. On the 28th Lord Kitchener walked round the troops, and on Sunday, 2nd March, the Battery retired a few miles north to Majoors Drift, where a telegram of congratulation was received from the Secretary of State for War. From here they started to drive the loose Boers into the position for a third drive, being part of a force of 10,000 men made up of columns of Barker, Elliot, Lawley and Rimington. Sweeping northwards, the Battery passed through Leuuwkop, Tafelkop, and then

THE STORY OF "G" TROOP. 87

swung eastwards towards Botha's Pass to Vrede and then north over the Klip River at Grausvlei to Alleman's Nek, where orders were received by Keir, to entrain his command for the western Transvaal. This change of plan was occasioned by the news of two defeats in those parts, namely, that of Lord Methuen at Tweebosch on the 7th March, at the hands of De la Rey when the British General was made prisoner, and the capture of a convoy by the same leader a few days previously. On the 13th, G and O Batteries entrained at Volksrust and started at midnight. They moved up the line through Standerton to Heidelberg where horses were watered at 1.30 p.m. twenty-four hours after starting, and again at Bramfontein. They reached Klerksdrop at 6.30 a.m. on the 15th, where many columns were assembled, and the Royal Artillery Mounted Rifles passed under the command of General Walter Kitchener. At this place Lieutenant Fulton left the Battery on promotion, and Lieutenant Sherbrooke joined.

THE WESTERN TRANSVAAL, 1902.

There now commenced what was perhaps the biggest drive of the war. About 16,000 British troops under Rawlinson, Kekewich, Walter Kitchener and Rochfort were concentrated in or near Klerksdorp ready to strike at Delarey. The Boer commanders were reported to be lying about thirty miles west of the Schoon Spruit, the stream on which Klerksdorp stands, and which joins the Vaal south of that town. It was decided therefore to move the columns, minus their baggage, by night to the westwards, deploy them on a line from Lichtenberg to the Vaal and sweep the Boers eastwards towards the Schoon Spruit. The columns moved at nightfall (6.45 p.m.) on Sunday, 23rd March. It was a clear moonlight night, and Keir's column, with which was the battery, marched straight through the hostile territory and reached Cypher Ghat, forty miles away, at 4.40 a.m. having unwittingly passed close to Kemp's commando of 350 men and two guns which was resting at Klipfontein. This leader, alarmed by the sounds of Keir's and Lowe's columns trekking past him, one on either side, saddled up and made good his escape before the net was closed. At 5 a.m. on the 24th, the line was formed and the drive was carried back as far as Rhenoster Hoek. The drive produced 165 prisoners, three guns and two pom-poms. It might have been productive of greater results but Delarey and Steyn with a few followers escaped early. Kemp slipped away as we have seen, and Liebenberg, after being for many hours in the toils, managed to squeeze through one of the unavoidable gaps in the line.

At 4.30 p.m. a terrific hail storm swept over the country, and the men, weary, hungry and without cloaks, were drenched to the skin. About 5 p.m. a welcome guide arrived at the column and led it to its bivouac about five miles to the northwards. The troops reached it at 6.30 p.m. The battery is calculated to have covered one hundred miles in the twenty-four hours. One horse died from cold and exhaustion during the night. On the 26th Keir's column returned to Klerksdorp. The next two days were spent in refitting and in discussing the many rumours of peace which flew around the camp, and this time there was some justification for them. Before they were to materialise, however, another action was to be fought.

Delarey's actual position was not known, but it was certain that he had concentrated his commandos to the westward of Klerksdorp, and Kitchener moved his forces, also more or less concentrated, against him. Owing to the lack of definite information the columns were ordered to move to various points and form entrenched camps as bases for further operations, and the one which concerns the battery, namely, Walter Kitchener's, was ordered to march to Driekuil near the source of the Brak Spruit. At 5 a.m. on the 29th, the column (Lowe, Cookson and Keir) set out westward and after a hot march bivouacked at 4 p.m. It moved again at 3 a.m. next morning and reached Rietvlei at 10 a.m. The baggage, which had been left behind arrived two hours later. On the following morning Lowe went to Driekuil to form the camp, whilst Cookson, with his own and Keir's force, went forward along the Brak Spruit to clear up the

THE STORY OF "G" TROOP.   89

situation. Their force consisted of the Royal Horse Artillery Mounted Rifles (G, J, O, P, and T batteries) under Major Mercer Canadian Mounted Infantry, 28th Mounted Infantry, Damant's Horse, Kitchener's Fighting Scouts, two companies Yeomanry, two guns 78th battery and two pom-poms. After marching through thick bush and bad going they struck a spoor which they followed and soon had the news of 500 Boers and two guns. At 10 a.m. the enemy were sighted, and the force cantered along for about six miles in pursuit, which brought Damant, who was leading, to the farm of Boschbult. Boers then appeared all round and Cookson halted. Keir's Mounted Infantry (G and O) were out on the left flank south of the farm and the other corps to the north. P and T held a small farm west of Boschbult. The few wagons having arrived and outspanned, Keir withdrew to the almost dry bed of the spruit south of the farm. It was then that the Boers appeared in large numbers and opened fire, whilst four guns appeared on a brush-covered hill, 5,000 yards south-west of the camp, and took toll of the horses and mules of the river bed. Liebenberg led his commando out from behind three guns and charged Keir. He swerved off under the fire, crossed the river bed east of the farm and repeated the operation against P and T. Repulsed by this fire, he recoiled to the rising ground to the north from whence the Boers were directing their main attack, and overwhelmed some scattered Mounted Infantry in his retreat. The enemy gained some small success against the screen of Mounted Infantry who were retiring from the northern slopes, but otherwise his attack was a failure, and after two hours heavy fighting he drew off. Whether this was in accordance with the wishes of Delarey, who had just come up, or against them is not known. The idea at the time was that the Boer leader wished to renew the attack, but it was probable that he had news of the approach of reinforcements and did not wish to risk a big engagement. It is supposed that he had about 2,700 men and four guns at the time, and the force opposed to him numbered 1,700 and two guns, so the latter idea is probably correct. Delarey admitted 164 casualties. The

British force lost about 200. Of the battery Corporal Mackie was killed, and Captain Hurst, Australian Mounted Infantry, who was attached, and Gunner Griffiths were wounded. The casualties amongst the horses were heavy.

Next day General W. Kitchener with Lowe's brigade came up and the enemy retired. The general had heard from some of the dispersed Mounted Infantry that the force had lost heavily and the survivors had surrendered, and had telegraphed the news to Lord Kitchener. The latter showed the telegram to Colonel Sclater and remarked that he "did not think it was true as he did not believe the Horse Artillery would ever surrender."

At 2.30 p.m. the force moved back. It was now raining hard, the going was very deep and the wagons heavy with wounded. At 9 p.m., after covering twelve miles, when the waggons were scattered all over the veldt and many broken down, the column halted till dawn. The night was black as pitch and it was raining in torrents, so it must be considered lucky that the Boers did not follow up the force. Possibly they were in a similar plight, for next day the waggons were collected without molestation, and the force moved into the entrenched camp at Driekuil, to which place, in response to an urgent message, Rawlinson had already brought his command.

Sir Ian Hamilton now assumed supreme command of the forces in the western Transvaal and proceeded to deal with the remaining Boers by deploying his force along the Brak Spruit to the Hart River and preparing for a sweep to the south. The battery was with Keir on the left of this line, then came Lowe, Cookson, Rawlinson and Kekewich on the extreme right. In front was Kemp, Potgieter and Liebenberg with about 2,500 men. De la Rey had gone to meet the Transvaal delegates in Klerksdorp. In the operation which followed the battery took little part, for Kemp, after on April 10th, demonstrating in front of Walter Kitchener, moved rapidly westward and attacked Kekewich next day at Roodewal in a manner unusual with the Boers, namely, a mounted charge across the open plain. He

THE STORY OF "G" TROOP.

was defeated and Potgieter in leading the charge was killed. Rawlinson launched his column in pursuit, and Walter Kitchener was ordered to cut the retreat at Vleshkraal. The troops marched all day, but were unable to accomplish the task. When they reached Vleshkraal next morning Kemp was beyond pursuit. That day they returned to Kliprif, and next day, the 13th, to Oriekuil Camp.*

In the evening of the next day the troops moved twenty-four miles to Leeukop and on the 15th, in conjunction with Rochfort from the south, drove towards Klerksdorp capturing between them about a hundred prisoners.

There now followed a three days halt when Captain Gosling joined the Battery vice Stirling, and from now until May 5th, the battery spent its time between Klerksdorp, Driekuil and Orebeejeesfontein, a camp situated midway between the two.

On the 5th, the battery set out on the last drive when Ian Hamilton, distributing his forces north and south through Korannafontein, drove the remaining Boers against the Vryburg-Mafeking line of blockhouses.

The Battery reached Vryburg on the 11th May, and bivouacked on the west side of it in a place where there was neither water nor grazing for the horses. Nearly four hundred Boers were captured on this day.

On the 15th, the troops retraced their steps, and on the 22nd the Battery made its last "war trek" into the environs of Klerksdorp, accompanied by the familiar music of a thunderstorm. It remained here until the declaration of peace on the 1st of June.

On June 4th, General Walter Kitchener set out to receive the surrenders in the western Transvaal. Major Mercer commanded his escort and the Battery formed a portion of it. The mission moved by Ventersdorp and Tafelkop to Doornkop where Delarey, Kemp, Liebenberg, Van der Merwe and over a thousand burghers laid down their arms. Then through the beautiful country of the Marico via Kleinfontein to Waterkloof

* Kekewich captured 20 prisoners. 2 guns and 1 pom-pom. 96 Boers were killed.

where Celliers surrendered. It returned through Lichtenburg and Googedacht reaching Klerksdorp on the 13th, the last week having been cold and wet.

On the 20th June orders were received for the Royal Horse Artillery Mounted Rifles to break up and next day P and R batteries marched for Pretoria, and T battery entrained for Bloemfontein. Next day G, J, and O batteries started on their march up the railway line to Elandsfontein (Germiston) which they reached on the 28th. On the 2nd July, Major Mercer left for England on leave pending promotion, and on the 8th August the battery left by train for Durban and embarked there, on the 14th, on H.M. Indian transport "Ionian," having been in South Africa nearly three years and nine months. It had marched 4,667 miles with guns and 1,076 as Mounted Rifles, and fired 5,059 shell.

The honours granted to the officers were as follows:—Major (then Lieutenant-Colonel) Bannatine-Allason received the brevet of Colonel; Major Mercer was made Companion of the Bath; Captain Stirling was promoted brevet Major, and Lieutenants Walthall and Delap received the D.S.O.

CONCLUSION.

During the time the battery was in India it maintained its reputation for smartness and efficiency. It was quartered for five and a half years at Bangalore, and for nearly four years at Secunderabad, and was commanded by Major S. E. G. Lawless from 1903 to 1906 and by Major L. Graham from 1906 to 1910 when Major H. M. Davson assumed command.

Whilst in Bangalore the battery had the honour of taking part in the Procession on the occasion of the visit of H.R.H the Prince of Wales on the 5th February, 1906, and in Secunderabad, on December 17th, 1910, from the Residency, Hyderabad, it fired the salute of welcome on the arrival of H.I.H. the Crown Prince of Prussia, and three days later led past the garrison when reviewed by his Imperial Highness. On the 16th

THE STORY OF "G" TROOP.　　93

October, 1911, it formed part of the escort to His Excellency the Viceroy (Lord Hardinge) from the Residency to the Chow Mahalla Palace when he visited the Nizam to greet him on his accession.

The battery left Secunderabad for England on Christmas Day, 1911, and arrived at Ipswich on the 17th January, 1912, having been on foreign service for over twelve years.

LIST OF OFFICES AND STAFF SERGEANTS

OF THE G BATTERY, ROYAL HORSE ARTILLERY WITH THEIR STATIONS,

From the Foundation of the Battery to the present time.

DATE.	DESIGNATION.	COMMANDER.	CAPTAIN.	LIEUTENANTS.		STAFF SERGEANTS.	STATIONS.
1801		C. B. Fisher,[2] capt.	F. Walker.*	H. D. Ross.[1]*	A. Wall.	J. Bruce.	Mallow.
1802		W. Bathwick,	R. Buckner.[6]	"	"	J. Lock.	Woolwich.
1803		A. S. Frazer,[3] capt.	J. Hawker.[5]				
1804		"	J. M. Close.	W. D. Nichols.	C. Rooke."	A. Braid.	Warley.
1805		"	N. W. Oliver.*	"	"	J. Spirler.	"
1806	G. Troop.	"	"	"	"	J. Hillhouse.	Colchester. Wareham, Christ-church.
1807		"	A. C. Mercer.*			"	South America.
1808		"	"	E. Sabine.[2]*§	W. Swabey.	W. Kirkwood.	Woolwich.
1809		"	"	"	T. F. Strangways.	J. Hale.	Woodbridge.
1810		Bt. Major,	"	"	"	"	"
1811		"	"	"	"	"	"
1812		"	T. French.	G. B. Smyth.	"	H. Parsons.	"
1813		Bt. L. Colonel,	"	"	"	"	"
1814		"	W. Bell.	J. Hinks.	W. B. Ingilby,[2]*	"	Colchester.
1815		Sir A. Dickson,[1]§ K.C.B., Bt. Lt. Col.	H. M. Leathes.	"	J. F. Briton.	"	Netherlands, France
1816		"	E. G. Wallcott	"	J. J. Chapman.	"	France.
1817		"		"	"	"	"

References: [1] =G.C.B. [2] =K.C.B. [3] =K.C.M.G. [4] =K.C.V.O. [5] =C.B. [6] =K.C.H. [7] =C.M.G. [8] =D.S.O. *=Col. Commandant, R.A. §=President of the Royal Society.

DATE	DESIGNATION	COMMANDER	CAPTAIN	LIEUTENANTS			STAFF SERGEANTS	STATIONS
1818		Sir A. Dickson, K.C.B., Bt. Lt. Col.	B. G. Wallcott	T. F. Strangways	J. Hinks	J. J. Chapman	H. Pearson	Woolwich
1819		"	"	"	"	"	"	2 guns to Glasgow
1820		"	"	"	"	F. Warde	"	"
1821		"	"	"	"	"	"	2 guns Glasgow to Leith
1822		"	Bt. Major	"	"	"	"	"
1823		A. Munro,⁶* Bt. Major	"	"	"	"	D. Burl	"
1824		F. G. Wallcott, Bt. Major	W. L. Lempriere	"	J. S. Rich	A. McBean	A. Chambers	2 guns rejoined Bland Bridge
1825								
1826	F. Troop.	"	T. F. Strangways	G. H. Pemberton	"	"	"	Athlone
1827		"	"	"	"	"	"	"
1828		"	"	"	"	"	"	Dublin
1829		"	"	"	G. James	"	"	Woolwich
1830		"	"	N. T. Lake,⁶	A. Tulloch.⁵	B. Cuppage.²*	J. Ledgerwood	2 guns to Bristol Woolwich
1831		"	"	"	"	"	"	Woolwich
1832		"	"	"	"	"	"	Leeds
1833		"	"	"	"	"	"	Newcastle
1834		"	"	"	"	"	"	"
1835		"	"	"	"	J. H. Cockburn	"	"
1836		W. Dunn	A. McBean	W. R. Nedham	Honble R. F. Hancock	C. V. Cockburn	R. Hall	Bland Bridge
1837								
1838		M. Louis	E. Trevor	"	"	"	E. Stainsbury	Limerick
1839		"	"	T. W. de Winton	P. R. Cooks	"	"	Dublin
1840		"	F. Holcombe	H. L. Gardiner.⁵*	"	"	M. McGregor	Woolwich
1841		A. McBean	A. H. Frazer	"	"	A. T. Phillpots.*	"	"
1842		"	"	"	"	"	"	"
1843		"	"	"	A. S. Somerset	Honble R. C. Spencer	"	"
1844		"	G. Sandham	"	"	"	W. Brooks	Leeds
1845								
1846		"	H. G. Ross, Bt. Major	W. F. Smith-Neill	"	J. D. Shakspear	J. Fenton	"
1847		"	G. Wilder	E. M. Reilly,⁵	A. E. H. Anson.³	"	H. Saffray	Newcastle
1848		W. R. Gilbert.⁵	"	"	"	"	W. Choriton	Portobello
1849		"	"	"	"	"	W. Kelly	Limerick
1850		"	"	"	"	J. F. L. Baddeley	J. Robinson	Portobello
1851		"	"	"	"	R. J. Hay.²*	J. Stevens	"
1852		"	J. Turner.⁵	"	G. H. Colomb	"	"	Portobello

References: ¹=G.C.B. ²=K.C.B. ³=K.C.M.G. ⁴=K.C.V.O. ⁵=C.B. ⁶=K.C.H. ⁷=C.M.G. ⁸=D.S.O. *=Col. Commandant, R.A.

DATE.	DESIGNATION.	COMMANDER.	CAPTAIN.	LIEUTENANTS.	STAFF SERGEANTS.	STATIONS.
1853	F. Troop (Continued)	"	Hon'ble E. T. Gage.[5]	"	G. Leeds, "	Woolwich.
1854		Bt. Major, (C. C. Young,)	F. S. Seale.	W. H. Goodenough.	"	Canterbury.
1855		C. L. D'Aguilar,[1]* Bt. Lt. Colonel,	H. Peel Yates.[5]*	H. P. Phelips.	E. Markham,[2]*	"
1856		"	"	F. Lyon.	W. Wookay.	Aldershot.
1857		Hon'ble D. M.	"	"	J. Wilkinson.	Woolwich to India.
1858	F. Battery, Horse Bde.	Fraser.	H. T. Arbuthnot.[5]	A. W. Burnaby.	A. K. Rideout.[5]	Oude.
1859		"	W. H. Goodenough.[2]		O. Orme.	Meerut.
1860		"	G. B. B. Hobart.	Hon'ble A. Stewart,	J. Wilkin.	"
1861	F. Battery,	"	"	A. Ford.[5]	"	"
1862	1st Horse	"	F. Lyon.	"	"	Woolwich.
1863	Brigade.	"	"	"	"	"
1864		A. S. Greene.[5]	"	Hon'ble A. Stewart,	T. B. Hamilton.	Dublin & Newbridge
1865		Bt. Major,	"	"	J. Drummond.	"
1866		"	J. M. Murray.[2]	V. Wing.	W. Garlick.	Dublin.
1867	C. Battery,—B. Brigade.	F. T. Whinyates.	"	"	"	"
1868		"	"	G. Best, "	"	Woolwich.
1869		"	"	"	H. R. G. Browne.	"
1870		"	"	J. R. Slade.[2]*	"	Canterbury.
1871		"	F. B. Knox.	"	"	"
1872		"	"	"	W. Hunter.	Aldershot.
1873		H. J. Holes.	Hon'ble A. Stewart,	H. Torkington.	J. Wilkin. Redmond (S.M.)	"
1874		F. G. Warren.[7]	W. F. M. Hitchinson*	L. Parsons.	Wingards, (Q.M.S.)	Woolwich to India.
1875		"	A. W. Anstruther.	"	F. C. Clarke.	G. Smith, (S.M.)
1876		"	L. J. A. Chapman.	"	"	Lucknow.
1877		"	T. J. Jones.	"	"	"
1878		W. J. Finch.	"	"	J. A. Grieve.	G. Gurney, (S.M.)
1879			S. V. Mackenzie.	"		J. S. Fletcher, (Q.M.S.)
1880	G. Battery,—A. Brigade.		T. R. Disney.	G. H. W. Beaumont		Morar.
1881		H. de G. Warter.	J. M. S. Brunker.	E. C. Hawkshaw.	J. Birch, (Q.M.S.)	"
1882		"	P. K. L. Beaver.	"	J. L. Keir.[5]	Meerut.
1883		"	C. H. Atchison.	E. A. Lambart.	F. Hinton, (S.M.)	"
1884		L. W. Taylor.	H. S. Dalbiac.	R. M. B. F. Kelly.[5,8]	"	"
1885		"	C. E. Goulburn.[3]	"	H. H. Clark.	"
1886		"	"	R. A. Stewart,	"	Ambala.
1887		"	"	"	J. U. Coates.	"
1888		O. B. Wickham.	F. E. A. Hunter.	P. H. Slee.	J. Birch, (S.M.)	"

References: ¹ = G.C.B. ² = K.C.B. ³ = K.C.M.G. ⁴ = K.C.V.O. ⁵ = C.B. ⁶ = K.C.H. ⁷ = C.M.G. ⁸ = D.S.O. * = Col. Commandant, R.A.

G. Battery

DATE	DESIGNATION	COMMANDER	CAPTAIN	LIEUTENANTS		STAFF SERGEANTS	STATIONS
1889		R. H. Wallace	C. Prescott-Decie	H. M. Ferrar		J. Howard, (Q.M.S.)	Dorchester
1890		"	"	"		W. Palmby, (Q.M.S)	"
1891		H. V. Hunt	J. F. Manifold.[7]	"		J. Jowett, (S.M.)	Aldershot
1892		"	H. A. Chapman	G. C. Fordyce		J. Stammes, (Q.M.S.)	"
1893		"	"	"	Buchan	" (S.M.)	"
1894		"	"	H. L. Powell		"	"
1895		R. Bannatine-	G. H. McLaughlan	"		W. Havern, (Q.S.M.)	Woolwich
		Allason.[5]	P. G. Best	"		"	"
1896		"	H. L. A. Jenkinson	C. Behrens		"	"
1897		"	"	"		"	"
1898		"	"	E. C. W. D.	W. P. Monkhouse	"	St. John's Wood
1899		"	"		M. R. F. Courage	"	"
1900		"	E. C. Cameron	B. G. Buchanan	Walthall.[8]	W. Dinness	South Africa
1901		H. F. Mercer.[5]	E. H. T. Parsons	J. D. B. Fulton	W. L. Foster.[8]	Offer, (S.S. Far.)	"
1902		"	"	"	H. H. Tudor	Bland, (S.M.)	"
					J. E. C. Livingstone-		
					Learmonth		
1903		"	C. Stirling	N. H. C. Sherbrooke	E. F. Calthrop	"	Bangalore
1904		"	S. F. Gosling		A. M. Fox.[8]	"	"
1905		S. E. G. Lawless	E. J. R. Peel	A. O. Boyd	E. W. M. Cuning-	"	"
1906		"	"		hame	"	"
					H. Cornes		
1907		L. Graham	J. G. Dennistoun	T. C. Sinclair	A. H. D. West	Shrabb, (S.M.)	Trimulgherry
1908		"	G. R. V. Kinsman	"	C. W. Spinks	Mayson, (Q.M.S.)	"
1909		"	E. W. Furse	H. G. Luah-Wilson	A. W. van Strau-	Body, (Q.M.S.)	"
					benzee	Pilgrim, (Q.M.S. Far.)	
1910		H. M. Davson	L. M. Goldie.[8]	J. K. L. Fitzwilliams	C. de B. Gidley	F. James, (S.M.)	"
1911		"	"	"	P. S. Rostron	Simmonds	"
					G. H. R. Blount	(S.S. Far.)	
1912		"	R. G. Finlayson	"		Baldwin, (S.S. Far.)	Ipswich
1913		"	H. E. Hambro	"	J. H. Nunn		"
1914		"	C. W. D. Uniacke	R. H. Carrington	T. F. Sandeman		"

References: [1] = G.C.B. [2] = K.C.B. [3] = K.C.M.G. [4] = K.C.V.O. [5] = C.B. [6] = K.C.H. [7] = C.M.G. [8] = D.S.O. * = Col. Commandant, R.A.

APPENDIX II.

A. C. MERCER.

Captain Mercer was the second son of General Mercer, R.E., and was born in 1783. He was commissioned from the R.M. Academy at the age of sixteen and was sent to Ireland at the time of the Rebellion. In 1808 he served with Whitelock's expedition to Buenos Ayres. He joined "G" Troop in 1807, and commanded it throughout the Waterloo Campaign. In 1824 he was ordered to Canada, being then a brevet major.

As Lieut.-Colonel in 1837 he commanded the Artillery at Nova Scotia during the time of dispute over the Maine boundary line. He subsequently commanded the garrison at Dover and the 9th brigade of Field Artillery. He became Major General in 1854: General on 9th February, 1865: and Colonel Commandant R.A. in 1859.

He died at Cowley Cottage, Exeter in 1868.

INDEX.

A.

Aasvogelkop 71
Abbéville 24
Aberdeen (Cape Colony) 6
Abonsdam 48
Abraham's Kraal 71
Achmuty, Brig.-Gen. Sir J....3, 4, 5
Airaines 24
Airlie, Colonel, Lord 42
Albrecht ....40, 42, 46, 47, and 48
Aldershot 38
Alderson's Mounted Infantry 55,
   58, 61, 62, 68, 76 and 77
Alexandersfontein 48
Allahabad 27, 28
Alleman's Nek 87
Allenby 76
Alumbagh 28
Ameathee Fort, taken (1858) 31
America, South, operations in,
   (1807) ....4—6
Amsterdam (S. Africa) 77
Anson, Sir A. E. H., K.C.B., R.A. 95
Anstruther, Lieut. A. W., R.H.A. 96
Arbuthnot, Lieut. H. T., after-
   wards Maj.-Gen., C.B., 26, 28, 29,
   30, 31, 32, 33, 34 and 96
Argenteuil 24
Armament of "G" Troop (1873)
   38, (1888) 38, (1901) 64
Ashburner, Capt. 7th Fusiliers ... 73
Ash Vale 26
Avesnes, French army at 22

B.

Baddelay, Lieut. J. F. L., R.H.A. 95
Bairam Ghat 32
Balmoral 65
Balmoral coal mines 62
Bangalore 92
Bankee 33
Bankfontein 63, 64
Bannatine-Allason, Major R., C.B.,
   R.H.A. 39, 40, 41, 58, 60 (n.) 64,
   92 and 97
Baraitch 32
Barker 86
Barnard's Dam 69
Barragon, Ensenada of 3
Bauterlez 15
Bavai 22
"Bays" at Secundra 28
Bean 24
Beaufort West 67
Beaumont 24
Beaumont, Lt. G. H. W., R.H.A. 96
Beaver, Capt. P. K. L., R.H.A. ... 96
Beer Vlei 70
Behrens, Lieut. C., R.H.A. 97
Belgium campaign 8
Bell, Lieut. (afterwards General
   Sir Wm., K.C.B.) Adjt. "G"
   Troop 7, 8, 94

Belmont 44
Bennauwheid 48
Benaauwdenhoutsfontein 48
Beni Mahdoo 32, 33
Benningsen 7
Beresford, General
   captured Buenos Ayres, 1807 ... 2
   retired to Monte Video 2
Best, Lieut. G., R.H.A. 96
Best, Lieut. P. G., R.H.A. 97
Bethlehem 80, 82, 83
Bethune, Col. ...69, 70, 73, 76, 78, 81
Beyers 76
Bezuidenhout's Drift 82
Biddulphsberg 80
Binche 22
Birch, J., (S.M.) R.H.A. 96
Blackley, Lieut. C., R.H.A. 94
Blanc Mesnil 23
Bland, (S.M.) R.H.A. 81, 97
Bligdschap 82
Bloemfontein 52, 69, 71, 72, 92
Bloemspruit 52, 53, 54
Blood River Poort 80
Blount, Lieut. G. H. R., R.H.A... 97
Blücher 14, 22, 23
Blücher at Versailles 24
Bockenhout's Kloof Ridge 58
Body, (Q.M.S.) R.H.A. 97
Boer revival 65
Bombay 38
Borthwick, Major W., R.H.A....2, 94
Boschbult 89
Boschpoort 62
Bosch Rand 72
Bosch Rand Ridge 51
Boshkop Farm 60
Bosman's Kop 54
Botha, Genl. Christian 76, 80, 81, 82
Botha, Louis 57
Bothasberg 86
Botha's Drift 70
Botha's Pass 75, 87
Boyd, Lieut. A. O., R.H.A. 97
Braid, Staff-Sgt. A. 94
Braine, le Comte 12
Brakpan 54
Brakspruit 88, 90
Brakvlei 85
Bramfontein 87
Brandfort 54
Brandwater 79
Breton, Lieut. 10, 21
Breton, Lieut. J. F., R.H.A. 94
Briggs, Capt. 43
Bristol 25
British troops, exemplary behav-
   iour of 11
Britstown 67, 69
Broadwood's Brigade 44, 47, 48, 54,
   73, 78, 79, and 83
Bronkhurst Spruit 60, 62

INDEX.

Brooks, Staff-Sgt. W., R.H.A. 95
Brown, Staff-Sgt. W., R.H.A. 96
Brown's Drift 40
Browne, Lieut. H. R. Y., R.H.A. 96
Bruce, Lieut. E. J., R.H.A. 96
Bruce, Staff-Sgt. J., R.H.A. 94
Bruges 9
Brunker, Lieut. J. M. S., R.H.A. 96
Brunswickers 19, 21
Bryburg 91
Buchanan, Lieut. B. G., R.H.A.... 64
Buckner, Capt. R., K.C.H., R.H.A. 94
Buenos Ayres, Expedition to, 1807
 2, 3, 4, 5 and 6
Bulfontein 79
Bull's Troop 12, 17, 23
Burghersdorp 67
Burl, Staff-Sgt. D., R.H.A. 95
Burnaby, Lieut. A. W., R.H.A. ... 96
Burordiah 33
Butcher, Major, R.F.A. 69
Butler, Lieut. A. T., R.H.A. 97
Butler, Lieut. J. W., R.H.A. 94

C.

Calais 24
Calcutta (1857) 27, (1861) 34
Calthrop, Lieut. E. F., R.A. 64,
 68, 76, 77 and 79
Calvinia 67
Cambray captured 23
Cameron, Capt. E. C., R.H.A. 44,
 64, and 97
Campbell 28
Campbell, Col., K.R.R. 66
Campbell 76
Canadians in S. Africa 62
Canadian M.I. 89
Canterbury, "G" at 24
Carolina 76
Carrington, Lieut. R. H., R.H.A. 97
Cateau Cambresis, Wellington at 22
Catillon sur Sambre, Blücher at 22
Cavalry charge at Klip Drift 47
Cawnpore 28
Celliers, surrender of 92
Chambers, Staff-Sgt. A., R.H.A. ... 95
Chapman, Capt. H. A., R.H.A. ... 97
Chapman, Lieut. J. J., R.H.A. 94, 95
Chapman, Lieut. L. J. A., R.H.A. 96
Chenevière, "G" at 23
Chorlton, Staff-Sgt. W., R.H.A. ... 95
Chow Mahalla Palace 93
Christchurch, "G" at 2
Clark, Lieut. H. H., R.H.A. 96
Clarke, Lieut. F. C., R.H.A. 96
Cleaveland, Lieut. R. F., R.H.A. 94
Clinton 17
Close, Capt. J. M., R.H.A. 94
Clyde, Lord 28, 32
Coal Drift 79
Coates, Lieut. J. U., R.H.A. 96
Cockburn, Lieut. C. V., R.H.A. ... 95
Cocks, Lieut. P. R., R.H.A. 95
Colbert 15
Colchester, "G" at 2, 8
Colstream Guards at Magersfontein 42

Colesburg 67
Colesburg Bridge 70
Colomb, Lieut. G. H., R.H.A. 95
Colombes 24
Colville Young, Brevet Major 25
Commando Nek 57
Commando Spruit 74
Compeignes 23
Conolly, Capt. 69
Constantia 55
Convention of Paris 23
Cookson 88, 89, 90
Cork, "G" at 7
Cornell's Spruit 86
Cornes, Lieut. H., R.H.A. 97
Courage, Lieut. M. R. F., R.H.A. 97
Crauford, General 3, 5
Critchell, Gunner 29
Crocodile River 57
Crocodile Spruit Pass 59
Cronje, General A. P. ...46, 48, 49,
 50 and 78
Crumlin 36
Cuninghame, Lieut. E. W. M.,
 R.A. 80, 83, 84, 97
Cuppage, Lieut.-Genl. Sir B.,
 K.C.B., Col. Comdt., R.A. 95
Cypher Ghat 87

D.

D'Aguilar, Major Charles, afterwards Lt.-Gen. Sir Charles,
 K.C.B. 25
D'Aguilar, Lt.-Col. H. 27
Dalbiac, Capt. H. S., R.H.A. 96
Damant 86, 89
Dartnell, General 76
Davidson, Col. W. L., R.H.A. 39, 50
Davout 23
Davson, Major H. M. 92, 97
De Aar "G" at (1899) 39
De Aar, Herzog at 67
de Cetto, Capt. L. C., R.H.A. 96
Deerdeport 57, 59
De Kiel's Drift, passage of, by
 General French 45
Delagoa Bay 64
Delagoa Bay Railway 60
Delange's Drift 74, 75
Delap, Lieut., D.S.O., R.A.M.C. 43,
 50, 54, 79. and 92
De la Rey ...55, 57, 75, 87, 88, 89, 91
De Lisle's M.I. ...67, 73, 75, 78, 79, 83
Dendermonde 9
Dennistoun, Capt. J. G., R.H.A.... 97
Derby (S. Africa) 77
Deriabad 30
De Wet 45, 50, 65, 67, 68, 69, 70,
 71, 72, 75, 78, 80, 82, 83, 85, and 86
Dewetsdorp 68
De Winton, Lieut. F. W., R.H.A. 95
Diamond Hill 58, 60
Dickson 58, 62, 63
Dickson, Bt. Lt.-Col. Sir Alexander, G.C.B., K.C.H., R.A. 7, 8,
 14, 94 and 95
Dinness, Staff-Sgt. W., R.H.A. ... 97
Discipline (1856) 26

INDEX. 101

Disney, Capt. T. R., R.H.A. 96
Doadpore 31
Dommett, Gunner 29
Doornberg 72
Doornkloof 83
Doornkop 56, 63, 65, 66, 83, 91
Doornkraal 57, 59
Dorchester 38
Dragoon Guards, 3rd ...69, 72, 73, 75
Dragoon Guards, 6th 3
Dragoon Guards, 7th 72, 73, 83
Dragoon Guards, King's 10, 69, 73, 74, and 83
Driefontein 51, 56
Driekuil 88, 90, 91
Driekuil Drift 74
Drummond, Staff-Sgt. J., R.H.A. 96
Dublin Fusiliers 65
Duke of Cornwall's L.I. 65
Dundee (S. Africa) 77
Duneiah 30
Dunn, Major W., R.H.A. 95
Dupree's Laager 55
Du Toit 57
Durban 81, 82, 92

E.

Ecloo 9
Edendale 58
Elandsfontein 92
Elands River 57, 80
Elliot, General 72
Enslin Station 40
Ermeloo 76, 77, 80
Escars 23
Eshowe 81
Etreilles 23
Eustace, Maj.-Genl. Sir F. 76

F.

Faizabad, ...30, 32
Fanny's Home Drift 83
Fauresmith 71
Fenian Rebellion (1867) ...36, 37, 38
Fenton, Staff-Sgt. J., R.H.A. 95
Ferrar, Lieut. H. M., R.H.A. 97
Finch, Capt. W. J., R.H.A. 96
Finlayson, Capt. R. G., R.H.A. ... 97
Fisher, Capt. G., B. (afterwards Major-Genl. Sir George Bulteel Fisher, K.C.B.) 1, 2, 94
Fitzwilliams, Lieut. J. K. L., R.H.A. 97
Fletcher, J. S., (Q.M.S.) R.H.A.... 96
Flint, Col. E. M., R.A. (R.F.A.) 64, (R.H.A.) 73
Ford, Lieut. A., C.B., R.H.A. 96
Fordyce-Buchan, Lieut. G. C., R.H.A. 97
Forêt 23
Fort Itala 81
Fort Prospect 81
Foster, Lieut. W. L., D.S.O., R.H.A. 43, 51, 97
Fox, Lieut. A. M., D.S.O., R.H.A., 72, 79, 80, and 97
Frankfort 74, 82, 85, 86
Franks, Brig.-General... ......27, 28

Fraser, Capt. & Bt. Maj., Hon. David, M., R.H.A. 31, 32, 33, 96
Fraser, Major 超C., 7th Hussars... 34
Frasnes 14
Frazer, Capt. A. H., R.H.A. 95
Frazer, Capt. A. S., (afterwards Sir Augustus Frazer, K.C.B.), R.A. 2, 4, 6, 7, 8, 18, 94
French, General 44, 45, 47, 50, 56, 57, 58, 59, 61, 62, 63 76
French, Lieut. T., R.H.A. 94
French cavalry, charges at Waterloo 18, 19, 20
Froneman 46, 79
Fulton, Lieut. J. D. B., R.H.A. 64, 79, 83, 87, and 97
Furse, Capt. E. W., R.H.A. 97
Futtighur, Mahommed Hussein, Nawab of 34

G.

Gage, Capt. Hon. E. T., C.B., R.H.A. 96
Galwey, Col. (Madras Fusiliers) 32
Gardiner, Genl. Sir H. L., K.C.V.O., C.B., Col. Comdt., R.A. 95
Garges 23
Garlick, Staff-Sgt. W. 96
Garratt 86
Genappe 13, 15
Geneva Sizing 72
Germiston 92
Ghent 9
Ghistel 9
Gidley, Lieut. C. de B., R.H.A. ... 97
Gilbert, Capt. Walter R., C.B., R.H.A. 25, 95
Glasgow 25
Glen 53, 54, 79, 80
Goedelegen 82
Gogra River 30, 32
Goldie, Capt. M. L., D.S.O., R.H.A. 97
Golfe Juan, landing of Napoleon at, ... 8
Goodenough, Lieut. W. H., (afterwards Lt.-Gen. Sir William, K.C.B.) 26, 34, 96
Good Hope Farm 63
Googedacht 92
Goomtee 29, 30
Gordon 62, 63
Gordon 45, 47
Gosling, Capt. S. F., R.H.A. ...91, 97
Gosselies 13
Gough 80, 81
Goulburn, Lieut. C. E., D.S.O., R.H.A. 96
Graham, Major L., R.H.A. 92, 97
Granvilliers 24
Grant, Sir Hope 30, 31, 32
Graspan 75
Grausvlei 87
Greatley, Lieut. T., R.H.A. 94
Greene, Bt. Major A. Sarsfield, C.B., R.H.A. 36, 96
Greytown 81
Grieve, Lieut. J. A., R.H.A. 96

INDEX.

Griffiths. Gunner, R.H.A. 90
Groenfontein 62
Grootvlei 78
Grouchy 15, 23
Gurney, G. (S.M.) R.H.A. 96

H.

Haasbroek 79, 80
Haine 22
Hale, Staff-Sgt. J., R.H.A. 94
Hall, Staff-Sgt. R., R.H.A. 95
Hambro, Capt. H. E., R.H.A. 97
Hamilton, Genl. Bruce 56, 69, 75
Hamilton, Genl. Ian 56, 59, 90, 91
Hamilton, Lieut. T. B., R.H.A. 36, 96
Hancock, Lieut. Hon. R. F., R.H.A. 95
Hanover Road 69
Hardinge, Lord 93
Harrismith 75, 78, 80, 81, 82, 83, 86
Hart River 90
Harwich 8
Havern. Q.M.S., R.H.A. 56, 97
Hawker, Capt. J., C.B., R.H.A. ... 94
Hawkesley, Lieut. J. P. V., R.H.A. 79, 83, 97
Hawkshaw. Lieut. E. C., R.H.A. 94
Hay. Lieut.-Genl. Sir R. J., K.C.B., Col. Comdt., R.A. 95
Headquarters Hill 40
Heidelberg 87
Heilbron 74, 78, 85, 86
"Hell" 66
Henniker-Major, Maj. (Coldstream Guards) 42
Herzog, Commandant 67
Hickes, Capt. H. J., R.H.A. 96
Highland Brigade 40
Hillhouse, Staff-Sgt. J., R.H.A. ... 94
Hinks, Lieut. J., R.H.A. 7, 21, 22, 94, and 95
Hinton, F., (S.M.) R.H.A. 96
Hitchings, Surgeon 24
Hoare, Major, 4th Hussars 73
Hobart, Lieut. G. B. B., R.H.A. 96
Hoek 85
Holcombe, 2nd Capt. F., R.H.A. 25 and 95
"Holmesdale" Transport 34
Hol Spruit 86
Honeynest Kloof 43
Honourable East India Company, end of 31
Hopetown 70
Horne, Maj. 7th Hussars, drowned 33 and 34
Horsford, Brigadier, C.B. 30
Houdenbek Hill 53
Hougoumont 17
Houssière 13
Hout Nek 72
Houwater 70
Howard. J., Q.M.S., R.H.A. 97
Hunt, Major H. V., R.H.A. 38, 97
Hunter, Capt. F. E. A., R.H.A. ... 96
Hunter. Lieut. W., R.H.A. 96

Hurst, Capt., Australian M.I. ... 90
Hussars, 7th 27, 30, 31, 33
Hussars, 10th 44, 49
Hussars, 14th 63
Hussars 18th 65
Hutchinson, Maj.-Genl. W. F. M., Col. Comdt., R.A. 96
Hutton, General 54, 55, 56, 57, 58, 59, 60, 61, and 62
Hyderabad 92
Hydergurgh 32

I.

Imperial Yeomanry 73
India. Government of, taken over by Crown 31
Indian Mutiny ....25—31
Ingilby, Lieut. (afterwards Gen. Sir W B., K.C.B.) 7, 10, 24, 94
Inniskillings 10
Intha 32
"Ionian," Transport 92
Ipswich 93
Irish Fusiliers 61, 62
Issy 23

J.

James, Lieut. G., R.H.A. 95
James, (S.M.) R.H.A. 97
Jeffreys, Colonel 68
Jenkinson. Capt. H. L. A., R.H.A. 39, 44 and 97
Johannesburg 56, 60
Jones, Capt. T. J., R.H.A. 96
Jowett, J., (Q.M.S.) R.H.A. 97
Jumna, H.M.S. 38

K.

Kaffir River 72
Kalkheuvel 57
Kameelfontein 49, 57, 58, 61
Karee Siding 53, 80
Keir, Col. J. L., R.H.A., 85, 87, 88, 90 and 96
Kekewich, Colonel 87, 90
Kellermann 15, 18
Kelly, Lieut. R. M. B. F. (afterwards Col. (temp. Brig.-Gen.) C.B., D.S.O., R.A.) 96
Kelly, Staff-Sgt. W., R.H.A. 95
Kemp, ...76, 87, 88, 90, 91
Kimberly, ride to 45
Kinsman, Capt. G. E. V., R.H.A. 97
Kirkwood, Staff-Sgt. W., R.H.A. 94
Kitchener's Fighting Scouts 89
Kitchener, Gen. Walter 87, 88, 90, 91
Kitchener, Lord ...68, 77, 86, 88, 90
Kitchener's Kopje 49, 50
Kleinbrach Kuil 70
Kleinfontein 91
Klein Vet River 72
Klerksdorp 79, 87, 88, 90, 91, 92
Klerksdorp Road...................... 55
Klip Drift 46
Klipfontein 56, 64, 87
Klip Kraal Drift...................... 46
Kliprif 91

INDEX.

Klip River ...56, 74, 75, 87
Klopfontein ... 45
Knighton ... 5
Knox, Gen. Sir Wm. ...57, 76, 77
Knox, Lieut. W. B., R.H.A. ... 96
Koffy Spruit ...61, 62
Komeboog Spruit ... 78
Koodoosrand Drift ...49, 50
Kooli, Fort ... 32
Koomati Poort ... 57
Koornspruit ...54, 72
Korannafontein ... 91
Kraankuil ... 70
Kritzinger ... 67
Kroonstadt 55, 72, 74, 75, 76, 77, 83, and ... 85
Kruger, President, flight of ... 64

L.

La Belle Alliance ... 18
Ladybrand ...67, 79
Ladysmith ...80, 81, 82
La Haie Sainte ... 16
Lake, Lieut. N. T., C.B., R.H.A. ... 95
Lake Chrissie ... 76
Lambart, Lieut. E. A., R.H.A. ... 96
Lambert's Bay ... 67
Lammerkop ... 66
Lancers, 9th ...28, 41, 47
Lancers, 12th ...41, 42, 44
Lancers, 16th ... 47
Landrecies ... 23
Laon, Soult at ...22, 29
La Tour ... 12
Lawless, Maj. S. E. G., R.H.A. 92 and ... 97
Lawley ... 86
Leathes, Lieut. H. M., R.H.A. 8, 21, and ... 94
Ledgerwood, Staff-Sgt. J. ... 95
Leeds ... 25
Leeds, Staff-Sgt. G. ... 96
Leeukop ...75, 86, 91
Leeuwpoort ... 61
Leicester Regiment ... 65
Leith ... 25
Lempriere, Capt. W. L., R.H.A. ... 95
Leveson-Gower, Brig.-Gen. ... 4
Lewis, Deputy Secretary at War... 3
Lewis, Miss, m. Gen. Whitelocke 3
Lichtenberg ...87, 92
Liebenberg ...88, 89, 90, 91
Life Guards ... 10
Light Dragoons 9th ... 3
                17th ...3, 4
                20th ... 3
                21st ... 3
Ligny ...14, 16
Lindley ...75, 76, 83, 85
Lindsay, Major Walter F. L., (afterwards Maj.-Gen., C.B., D.S.O.) ... 41
Line Regiments: —
  5th Regiment ... 3
  14th Foot ... 2
  36th Regiment ... 3
  38th   ,, ... 3
  40th   ,, ... 3

41st   ,, ... 4
42nd   ,, ... 15
45th   ,, ...3, 5
49th   ,, ... 3
52nd   ,, ... 36
54th   ,, ... 3
60th Rifles ... 65
87th Regiment ...3, 5
88th   ,, ...3, 5
89th   ,, ... 3
92nd   ,, ... 15
95th   ,, ... 3
Liniers General ...4, 5, 6
Livingstone-Learmouth, Lieut. J. E. C., R.H.A. ...57, 64, 97
Lloyd, Capt., R.H.A. ... 24
Lloyd, Capt., 21st Lancers ... 73
Lock, Staff-Sgt. J. L., R.H.A. ... 94
Locke - Elliot, Major-Gen., C.B., D.S.O. ...72, 73, 75, 77, 79, 83, 86
Loubaken Hill ... 58
Louis, Capt. M., R.H.A. ... 95
Louis XVIII., Army of ... 9
"G" Battery finding guard for, 9
Lowe ...76, 78, 79, 83, 87, 88, 90
Lucknoff ... 71
Lucknow ...28, 29, 30, 32, 34
Lush-Wilson, Lt. H. G., R.H.A.... 97
Lyon, Capt. F., R.H.A. ... 96
Lyon, Lieut. Francis ...26, 31, 33
Lyttelton, Major-Gen. The Hon. N. ...64, 65, 69

M.

Maberly, Major, R.H.A. ... 43
Maberly, Col., R.A. ... 28
McBean, Capt. A., R.H.A. ... 95
McDonald, Major ...12, 13, 14
McGregor, Staff-Sgt. M., R.H.A. ... 95
Mackenzie, Lieut. S. V., R.H.A.... 96
Mackie, Corporal, R.H.A. ... 90
McLaughlin, Capt. G. H., R.H.A. 97
Macleod, J., D.A.G. of Artillery 1, 2
McNeil, Col., Fenian Rebellion (1867) ... 37
Madras Fusiliers ... 31
"Madras," H. E. I. C's 88. ... 27
Madras Light Cavalry, 6th ... 33
Magersfontein ... 40
Mahon, Col. ...60, 61
Mahon, Col. Hon. T. ... 4
Majoor's Drift ... 86
Mallow, "G" Troop formed at ... 2
Manifold, Captain J. F., C.M.G., R.H.A. ... 97
Marico ... 91
Maritzberg ... 82
Markham, Lieut. E., (afterwards Lt.-Gen. Sir Edwin, K.C.B.) 26, 29, and ... 96
Maubeuge ... 22
Mayson, (Q.M.S.) R.H.A. ... 97
Meerut ... 38
Meguidia Fort captured ... 33
Merbe Braine ... 17
Mercer, Capt. A. Cavalié, R.A. 7 8, 11, 12, 13, 14, 16, 17, 21, 24. 94
Mercer's Career. Appendix II.

INDEX

Mercer, Major H. F., c.b., R.H.A.
54 (note), 64, 85, 89, 91, 92 and 97
Merton Siding ... 40
Methuen, Lord ... 87
Meyer ... 86
Middelburg, 57, 62, 63, 64, 65, 67, and ... 68
"Middleton," Transport ... 35
Milhaud ... 18, 21
Mistquasfontein Drift ... 55
Modder River ... 39, 46, 51, 53, 54
Monkhouse, Lieut. W. P., R.H.A. 97
Mons, British Army at, (1815) ... 22
Montevideo ... 3, 6
Mont St. Jean ... 16, 17
Mooiplaats ... 76
Morar ... 38
Mounted Infantry, Canadian ... 89
    "   " 28th ... 89
Müller, Lieut. (Boer) ... 65
Munn, Major ... 61
Munro, Maj.-Genl. A., k.h., Col. Commandant, R.A. ... 95
Munshiguni Fort ... 28, 29
Murray, Lieut. J. M. ... 36, 96

N.

Naauwpoort ... 63, 69
Nahupara ... 32, 33
Nana Sahib ... 32, 33, 34
Napoleon ... 7, 23
Napoleon at Golfe Juan ... 8
Napoleon crosses Sambre ... 12
Natal ... 77, 80
Nawab Gunge ... 32
Nedham, Lieut. W. R., R.H.A. ... 95
Nels Farm ... 82
Nesle, birthplace of Blondel ... 23
Newcastle ... 77
New Zealand contingent in South Africa ... 55, 59, 61, 62, 70
Ney ... 18, 19, 21
Nichols, Lieut. W. D., R.H.A. ... 94
Nivelles ... 13
Ninove ... 9
Noailles Beavais, "G" at ... 24
Nooitgedacht ... 64, 79
Norvals Pont ... 69
Nunn, Lieut. J. H., R.H.A. ... 97

O.

Offer, (S.S. Far.) R.H.A. ... 97
Olifants River ... 63, 66
Olifants Vlei ... 55
Oliver, N. W., Col. Comdt. R.A. ... 94
Orange River ... 67, 70, 71
Orange River Station ... 70
Orebeejeesfontein ... 97
Oriekuil Camp ... 91
Orme, Staff-Sgt. O., R.H.A. ... 96
Osfontein ... 50
Ostend, "G" Troop at ... 8
Ostend, difficulties of disembarkation ... 8, 9
Oude, Begum of ... 32, 34
Onde, campaign of ... 29
Outram ... 28

Owen ... 79

P.

"P" Battery, R.H.A. ... 39, 44
Paardeburg Drift ... 49
Paardehoek ... 82
Pack ... 5, 15
Paget ... 65, 66
Palmby, W. (Q.M.S.), R.H.A. ... 97
Pau ... 63, 64
Paris, Convention of ... 23
Parsons, Capt. E. H. T., R.H.A. 64, 66, 68, 72 and ... 97
Parsons, Staff-Sgt. H., R.H.A. ... 94
Parsons, Lieut. L., R.H.A. ... 96
Parys ... 55, 73
Paso Chico ... 4
Payne, Col. ... 65
Pearson, Staff-Sgt. H., R.H.A. ... 95
Peel, Capt. E. J. R., R.H.A. ... 97
Pemberton, Lieut. G. H. ... 95
Phelips, Lieut. H. P. ... 26, 96
Philippeville, French army at ... 22
Phillpotts, Genl. A. T., Col. Comdt. R.A. ... 95
Pienaar ... 62
Pienaar's River ... 58
Piet Retief ... 77
Pietrusburg ... 71
Pilcher ... 60, 61
Pilgrim (Q.M.S. Far.), R.H.A. ... 97
"Pindari," SS. ... 39
Piré's cavalry at Waterloo ... 17
Pitman, Capt., 11th Hussars ... 73
Plessis Rust ... 79
Plumer, Colonel ... 69, 70, 71, 75
Poix ... 24
Poplar Grove, battle of ... 51
Porter's Brigade ... 50, 55, 58, 61
Potgieter ... 90, 91
Powell, Lieut. H. L., R.H.A. ... 97
Prescott-Decie, Lieut. C. ... 97
Pretoria ... 57, 60, 61, 62, 68, 76, 92
Prieska ... 67
Prince of Wales's Light Horse 69, 73
Prinsloo ... 40, 83, 84
Pulteney ... 76
Punjab Rifles, 5th ... 30, 31

Q.

Quaggafontein ... 83
Quatre Bras ... 13, 14
Quatre Bras, storm at ... 15
Quilmer ... 4

R.

Radcliffe, Lt. P. P. de B., R.H.A. 39, 97
Ramahatjes ... 72
Ramdam ... 45
Rampore Fort taken ... 31
Ramsay, Major ... 14, 17
Ramsden, Lieut. H., R.H.A. ... 97
Raptee River ... 29, 33
Rawlinson ... 87, 90, 91
Redmond (S.M.), R.H.A. ... 96
Reduccion ... 4
Rehora Fort taken ... 32

INDEX. 105

Reilly, Lieut. E. M., R.H.A. 95
Reitpan 79
Reitz 75, 78
Rhenoster Hoek 67, 88
Rhenosterkop 63
Rhenosterpoort 73
Rhenoster River 73, 79
Rich, Lieut. J. S., R.H.A. 95
Richmond Road 69
Rideout, Lieut. A. K., (afterwards Maj.-Gen. c.b.) 29, 31, 34, 96
Rietfontein 60
Riet River 46
Riet Vlei 60, 61, 88
Rimington 83, 86
Rio Chuelo 4
Roberts, Lord 53, 57, 59, 65
Robinson, Staff-Sgt. J., R.H.A. ... 95
Rochfort's Brigade 48, 87, 91
Rocket carriage, used by R.A. (1857) ......(note) 26
Rondeval Drift 47
Ronequières 13
Rooke, Lieut. C., R.H.A. 94
Roodeplats Farm 58, 59
Roodeval 90
Ross, Genl. Sir H. D., G.C.B., Col. Comdt. R.A. 94
Ross, Bt. Major H. G., R.H.A. ... 95
Rostron, Lieut. P. S., R.H.A. 97
Royal Artillery Mounted Rifles 85, 86, 87, 89 and 92
Royal Field Artillery:—
  5th Battery 85
  21st   ,, ... 65
  62nd   ,, ... 73
  63rd   ,, ... 80
  66th   ,, ... 56, 60
  75th   ,, ... 41
  78th   ,, ... 89
  82nd   ,, ... 73
  85th   ,, ... 65
Royal Horse Artillery:—
  Formed (1793) 1
  Discipline 26
  Subalterns 26
  Expenses (1856) 26
  Chestnut Troop 64
  "D" Troop 24
  "E"   ,, ... 27
  "G"   ,, see Table in appendix.
  "J" Battery 76, 85, 89, 92
  "M"   ,, ... 60
  "O"   ,, 45, 47, 55, 57, 58, 62, 72, 75, 85, 87, 89 and 92
  "P" Battery 39, 44, 47, 48, 49, 50, 53, 85, 89 and 92
  "Q" Battery 47
  "R"   ,, ...45, 47, 85, 92
  "T"   ,, ...47, 57, 58, 85, 89, 92
  "U"   ,, ... 47
  "V" Brigade ......(note) 16
Russell Sir William 32

S.

Sabine, Lieut. E., K.C.B., R.H.A. ... 94
Saffray, Staff-Sgt. H., R.H.A. 95
Saint Denis 23, 24

St. Gille 9
Saltzmans Farm 52
Sandeman, Lt. J. F., R.H.A. 97
Sandham, Capt. G., R.H.A. 95
Sannah's Post 54, 72
Sara Gunge 30
Schoon Spruit 87
Sclater, Colonel 90
"Scotland" 88. ......26 27
Scots Greys 10, 36
Scots Guards at Magersfontein ... 42
Scott, Sergt. R.H.A. 82
Seale, Lieut. F. S., R.H.A. 96
Secrora 32
Secunderabad 92, 93
Secundra, "G" Troop at 27, 28
Selimpore 28
Senekal 71
Senekal Rd. 80
Senne 13
Sevenoaks 2
Shakspear, Lieut. J. D., R.H.A. ... 95
Shanz Kraal 72
Sherbrooke, Lieut. N. H. C., R.H.A. 87, 97
Shoeman's Drift 73
Shrubb (S.M.) R.H.A. 97
Simmonds, (S.S. Far.) R.H.A. 97
Simonds, Lt. C. B., R.H.A. 97
Sinclair, Lt. T. C. 97
Slaagkraal Hill 51
Slade, Col. Sir J. R., K.C.B., Col. Comdt. R.A. 96
Slee, Lieut. P. H. 96
Smaaldeal 55, 77
Smith, G., (S.M.) R.H.A. 96
Smith, Lieut. W., R.H.A. 96
Smith, Lieut. W. C., R.H.A. 94
Smith-Dorrien 76
Smith-Neill, Lieut. W. F., R.H.A. 95
Smyth Capt. 21st Lancers 73
Smyth, Lieut. G. B., R.H.A. 94
Snyman, Commandant 58
Soissons, Soult at 23
Somerset, Lieut. A. S. 95
Somerset's (Lord Edward) Brigade 10, 13
Joined by "G" Troop 22
Sobraon 28
Soult 22, 23
South Australians 73
Spencer, Lt. Hon. R. C., R.H.A. ... 95
Spinks, Lt. C. W., R.H.A. 97
Spirter, Staff-Sgt. J., ... 94
Springfield Farm 54
Springs 60 76
Spytfontein 83
Stabberstswaag 83
Stainsbury, Staff-Sgt. E., R.H.A. 95
Stammas, J., (S.M.) R.H.A. 97
Standerton, ...75, 76, 87
Standerton Road 60, 61
Stanford, Staff-Sgt. W., R.H.A. ... 96
Stanger 81
Staveley, Capt. E., R.H.A. 96
Sterkwater 69
Stevens, Staff-Sgt. J., R.H.A. 95
Stewart, Capt. Hon. A., R.H.A. ... 96
Stewart, Lieut. R.A., R.H.A. 96
Steyn, John 52, 75, 82, 86, 88

INDEX.

Steyn (brother of President) 78
Steynesburg 67
Stirling, Bt. Maj. Chas. C.B., R.H.A. 72, 83, 91, 92, 97
Stisted, Capt. (7th Hussars) 34
Strangways, Lt. T. F., R.H.A. 94, 95
Strathnairn, Lord, Fenian Rebellion 36
Stridjpoort or Strydpoort 76, 86
Strytem 9, 12
Sultanpore 30
Swabey, Lieut. W., R.H.A. 94
Swaziland 76

T.

Tabaksberg 80
Tafelkop 86, 91
Talbot, Capt. F. S., R.H.A. 96
Tallaght 36
Taylor, Bombardier 28
Taylor, Capt. L. W., R.H.A. 96
Thabanchu 67
Tilsitt, Peace of 7
Tituspan 71
Torkington, Lieut. H., R.H.A. ... 96
Trevor, Capt. E., R.H.A. 95
Tucker's Division 45, 53, 54
Tudor, Lieut. H. H....39, 41, 42, 51, 97
Tugela River 81
Tulloch, Lieut. A., C.B., R.H.A. ... 95
Turner, Capt. J., C.B., R.H.A. 95
Tweebosch 87
Tweefontein 83

U.

Umballa 38
Uniacke, Capt. C. W. D., R.H.A. 97
Utrecht (S. Africa) 80
Uxbridge, Lord 15

V.

Vaal River 55, 73, 74, 79, 85, 87
Valsh River 78, 79
Vandamme 23
Vandeleur, Sir Ormsby 12
Van der Merwe 91
Van Straubenzee, Lieut. A. W., R.H.A. 97
Van Wyks Rust 55
Vechtkop 74
Ventersbloom 79
Ventersburg 72
Ventersdorp 91
Verneuil 23
Versailles 24
Vet River 54, 55, 72
Vierfontein 79
Viljoen, Ben 61, 62, 65
Viljoen's Drift 55
Villars Cauterets 23
Villiersdorp 74
Vivian, Sir Hussey 12, 13, 14
Vlakfontein 62
Vleshkraal 91
Volksrust 87
Vrede 87
Vredepoort Road 74
Vryheid 77, 81

W.

Wales, Prince of, christened (1842) 25
Walker, Genl. F., Col. Comdt. R.A. 94
Wall, Lieut. A., R.H.A. 94
Wallace, Major R. H., R.H.A. 38, 97
Wallcott, Capt. E. G., R.H.A. 94, 95
Walthall, Lieut. E. C. W. D., D.S.O., R.H.A. 39, 60, 61, 62, 63, 64, 66, 92 and 97
Warde, Lieut. R.H.A. 95
Wareham 2
Warley 2
Warren, Capt. F. G., C.M.G., R.H.A. 96
Warter, Capt. H. de G., R.H.A. 96
Waterkloof 91
Waterloo, battle of ......16—21
Waterloo campaign .... 8—21
Waterval 57
Waterval Drift 45, 54, 66
Waterworks (Sannah's Post) 72
Webber-Smith 17
Welgevonden 72
Wellington, Duke of 9, 12, 17, 22, 23
Wessels, General 78
West, Lieut. A. H. D., R.H.A. ... 97
Whinyates, Capt. F. T., R.H.A. 16, 36 and 96
Whitcroft, Corporal R.H.A. 82
Whitelocke, General ......2—7
Wickham, Major C. B., R.H.A. 38, 96
Wildebosch 79
Wilder, Capt. G., R.H.A. 95
Wilge River 62, 65, 74, 75, 78, 82, 86
Wilkin, Staff-Sgt. J., R.H.A. 96
Wilkins, Sergt., R.H.A. 29
Wilkinson, Staff-Sgt. J., R.H.A..... 96
Willowmore 67
Wilmot, Major E., R.H.A. 24
Wilmot, Lieut. E., R.H.A. 94
Wing, Lieut. V., R.H.A. 96
Winburg, ...72, 80
Wingards (Q.M.S.) R.H.A. 96
Witfontein 57
Witkop 80
Witpoort Ridge 61, 62
Wittebergen 79, 80
Witte Kopjes 79
Wolvekraal 49
Wonderfontein 63, 64
Wookay, Staff-Sgt. W., R.H.A. ... 96
Woolwich 2, 24, 25, 26, 34, 36

Y.

Yates, Capt. and Bt. Major H. Peel, C.B., R.H.A. 26, 28, 29, 30, 34 and 96
Yorkshire Light Infantry 76
Young, Capt. C. L., R.H.A. 96

Z.

Zand River 55, 78
Zand River Drift 72
Zilikats Nek 61, 62
Z.A.R.P. 55
Zululand 80
Zwavel Poort 60

www.ingramcontent.com/pod-product-compliance
Lightning Source LLC
Chambersburg PA
CBHW060838190426
43197CB00040B/2676